D1321879

Chaplaincy

Chaplaincy

The church's sector ministries

Edited by Giles Legood

CASSELL

Cassell
Wellington House, 125 Strand, London WC2R 0BB
370 Lexington Avenue, New York, NY 10017–6550
www.cassell.co.uk

First published 1999

British Library Cataloguing-in-Publication Data
A catalogue record for this book is available from the British Library

ISBN 0-304-70295-1

Typeset by SetSystems Ltd, Saffron Walden, Essex
Printed and bound in Great Britain by Biddles Ltd, Guildford and King's Lynn

Contents

The contributors

Gerald Arbuckle SM works with the Refounding and Pastoral Development organization in Sydney, Australia. His books include *Refounding the Church: Dissent for Leadership* and *Grieving for Change: A Spirituality for Refounding Gospel Communities.*

Paul Avis is General Secretary of the Council for Christian Unity of the Church of England, Sub Dean of Exeter Cathedral and Director of the Centre for the Study of the Christian Church. His books include *Authority, Leadership and Conflict in the Church* and *Faith in the Fires of Criticism: Christianity in Modern Thought.*

Denis Claringbull is National Moderator of the Industrial Mission Association and a Canon Emeritus of Birmingham Cathedral. He has been an Industrial Chaplain since 1961 and is now Founder Chairman of the Birmingham Centre for Business Ethics.

Robert Cooper is Assistant Chaplain to the Arts and Recreation in North-East England and Priest-in-charge of Sadberge.

Bill Down is assistant Bishop of Leicester and Priest-in-charge of Humberstone. Formerly General Secretary of the Missions to Seamen and later Bishop of Bermuda, he is an honorary Fellow of the Nautical Institute, and the author of *On Course Together: The Churches' Ministry in the Maritime World Today.*

Sophie Gilliat-Ray is a Research Fellow in the department of sociology at the University of Exeter. Her research has included the interface of publicly funded chaplaincy in prisons and hospitals and civil religion.

William Hall is Senior Chaplain to the Arts and Recreation in North-East England and an honorary Canon of Durham Cathedral.

Lyn Jamieson is Chaplain of the MetroCentre, Gateshead, and an honorary Canon of Durham Cathedral.

Keith Lamdin is Director of Training in the Diocese of Oxford and an honorary Canon of Christ Church Cathedral. He is the author of *Monday Matters.*

Giles Legood is Chaplain of the Royal Veterinary College, the Royal Free Hospital School of Medicine and University College London Medical School. He is co-author of *The Godparents' Handbook.*

David Lindsay is Chaplain to The Haberdashers' Aske's School, Hertfordshire. He was formerly Chaplain at the University of Keele.

Christopher Moody is Team Rector of Market Harborough. Formerly Chaplain of King's College, London, he is the author of *Eccentric Ministry: Pastoral Care and Leadership in the Parish.*

Georgina Nelson is Chaplain at St John's Hospital, Livingston.

Harry Potter is a barrister practising in criminal law and was formerly Chaplain of Aylesbury Young Offenders' Institution and Selwyn College, Cambridge. He is the author of *Hanging in Judgment: Religion and the Death Penalty in England.*

Anthony Russell is Bishop of Dorchester, and was formerly Director of the Arthur Rank Centre at the National Agricultural Centre. His books include *The Clerical Profession* and *The Country Parish.*

Michael Vincer is Chaplain of Manchester Airport. He was formerly an Area Secretary with the United Society for the Propagation of the Gospel (USPG) and a Minister in Secular Employment in Exeter, Devon.

Stephen Ware is a Chaplain in the Royal Air Force and is the RAF Director at the Armed Forces' Chaplaincy Centre, Amport House.

James Woodward is Master of the Lady Katherine Leveson Hospital, and Vicar of Temple Balsall. Formerly Chaplain of the Queen Elizabeth Hospital Birmingham, he is editor of *Embracing the Chaos: The Church's Response to AIDS* and author of *Encountering Illness.*

Barry Wright is Senior Chaplain to the Metropolitan Police and was formerly a Chief Inspector of Police and an honorary Canon of Southwark Cathedral.

Introduction

Why chaplaincy?

Until the industrial revolution, most people lived and worked in one place (parish) for most of their lives. Urbanization and new technology altered that forever: many began travelling in a way previously unknown and resided in a number of places during their lives. Neither the episcopal churches with their ancient parish systems, nor the Free churches with their congregational structures, altered, and as a consequence people's attachment to the church weakened. One of the attempts to respond to this change during the last fifty years has been the dramatic establishment and rise in the number of chaplaincies and chaplaincy posts. In recent years, whilst the church has had to re-adjust in its task of serving society, almost all its deliberations have focused on residential, or parish, ministry. Even recently published histories of the last hundred years of church life have largely ignored the work, witness and contribution made by clergy not working in parochial or congregational appointments. Clergy working in sector ministries, however, have much to contribute to the question of what roles the church should adopt in the future. This book is an attempt to explore some of the important issues which arise from the various contexts of the developing sector ministries. Sector ministers are paid to spend their working time with those who are not church members (those the church claims it most wants to reach). Paradoxically, it is chaplaincy posts which are often the first to be examined when questions of 'downsizing' (sometimes even called 'rightsizing') are being faced by the church, even though many of the institutions in which they serve (for instance, a university of 25,000 people) are the size of small towns.

There are, of course, significant numbers of women and men, ordained by the church to its ministry, not working in full-time, paid parochial or congregational posts. For centuries clergy have been employed in schools, universities and other sectors, for work which is not primarily concerned with their status as ordained members of the church. Historically many of these clergy were ordained into such work without having previously served in a locality-based ministry. Others have been ordained to serve in an unpaid, part-time capacity in a particular parish or congregation, and within the last generation such people have been known variously as non-stipendiary ministers (NSMs), local non-stipendiary ministers (LNSMs), ministers in secular employment (MSEs) or other similar titles.[1] Even within the church structures themselves, other clergy too are employed in such posts as directors of education, directors of training or as resources advisors: positions where it is not required that it is an ordained person who carries out the work. There is yet a further group of clergy who work in and for the church in a full-time, paid capacity in which their ordained status is essential to their work. Chaplains working with those who are deaf, for instance, fall within this category, although their work largely takes place within Christian communities. Some clergy work in chaplaincy as part of their parochial or congregational duties, or part-time for an honorarium. What unites the ministries examined in this book is that they are all full-time, paid clerical posts which are not centred on the residential, parochial system. Paid for by the church, or more commonly by the institution in which they are working, a number of these ministries have been written about in articles, pamphlets and books. It is hoped that, for the first time, in gathering a number of these experiences and reflections together, this book will serve as an introduction to the work of chaplaincy.

In noting the rise of such chaplaincies within the last fifty years some have asked 'What was it that chaplaincy could provide which could not be provided by the residential, parochial structure?' One immediate answer that can be given is that the church felt that it was necessary to have persons able to engage with the changing employment and institutional situations. It was felt that the parochial clergy working in the areas in which these institutions were set would be unable to do this, as they knew neither who people were nor where they could be found. As a consequence, it was deemed appropriate to appoint clergy specifically for this task and to ensure that they had no parochial or congregational responsibilities that might overburden them in this work. In the early days of this chaplaincy expansion, the experiences of chaplains in the Second World War were still fresh in people's minds. It was felt that these new chaplains might have a task similar to padres in the armed forces, who had become completely involved in the institution and were familiar with its language and way of life. The work of chaplains, then, has a particular orientation in a particular environment.

Some of the similarities with parochial clergy are easily made; both chaplains and residential clergy are concerned with pastoral care, spiritual nurture, leading worship and helping the laity in their mission in the world.[2] In each case, too, the task is the service both of the Christian community and of those who do not formally belong to it. However, despite these similarities there are a number of features that separate the two ministries. The differences lie in the environments within which each operates.

In no small part, one of the areas of confusion and tension has been the problems over naming or defining chaplaincy. In terms of nomenclature chaplaincy can be a minefield. In the early days of chaplaincy expansion the term 'specialized ministry' was used.[3] This rightly angered a large number of parochial clergy who felt that this term demeaned their own ministry, as if it was not itself in some way specialized. Acceptance of this term could lead to, 'specialists,' being seen as superior or more expert. To counter these objections the term 'non-parochial ministry' began to be used. This too brought its own problems, as chaplains now saw themselves being defined in relation to the parish or congregational model of ministry. They felt that the latter was seen as normative and their own ministry as in some sense deviant or abnormal. A term was thus arrived at which seemed not to insult any engaged in ministry, of whatever type, and which emphasized the rich variety of ministries within the church. 'Sector ministry' became widely used and accepted, as it simply defines the part (sector) in society in which the particular ministry is carried out (some chaplains, it should be noted, are dissatisfied with the term as they are well aware that the term may be meaningless to the large number of people who have never previously encountered the phrase). In 1983 a Church of England report entitled *Sector Ministries* gave the following definition: 'By the term sector we mean a slice of social or church life which can be identified as containing certain linked values, knowledge, skills and practices and forming an area of professionalism. Ministry within a sector will be carried out by lay or ordained persons who are of proven ability in the professional area and will bring to bear upon it the concerns of the Gospel, the teaching of the Church and its spiritual and pastoral care.'[4]

In this book, and in chaplaincy generally, it should be noted that the titles of chaplaincy posts can say much about how chaplaincy work is perceived in a particular sector. When, for instance, chaplaincy jobs are advertised it is interesting to read that posts are variously described as chaplain *to/of/at/in*. A post described as chaplain *to* might mean that the position is one funded by the church rather than the institution and that, consequently, the post-holder may be viewed as a guest in the sector. Alternatively a chaplain *of* may well be in a post funded by the institution itself, and the chaplain is therefore seen as part of the institution. A chaplain *at* is a more neutral term and it is harder to be certain how the chaplaincy role in such a place is understood. As a consequence, increasingly some chaplains are describing a post as chaplain *at*. Such descriptions have often been adopted in sectors such as hospitals where in recent years it has become popular to identify people by their names and the work they do rather than by the title they hold (doctor, professor, etc.). The description chaplain *at* also helps chaplains identify in closer ways with other members of the hospital staff who would not describe themselves as, for example, a nurse *of* the hospital but as a nurse *at* the hospital. We should not think from this, however, that chaplaincy job titles can always be understood in clear and certain ways, but it is the case that titles can often provide useful pointers as to how particular posts are understood and funded.

The penumbra of parochial and sector ministries

There are certain tensions that lie in the differences between parochial clergy and chaplains, not just those of naming. To serve as an introduction to the work of chaplaincy, it is useful for us briefly to name four of these, as they are not only worth considering in their own right but will also raise the topic of the theological underpinning of chaplaincy which forms the first chapter of the book.

1. Some parochial clergy have felt that their position is threatened, both specifically and generally, by the presence of chaplains. For hundreds of years the parish or local congregation has been the basic unit of the church's life and work. Sector ministry can be seen by some as contributing to the breaking down of the unity of the church and to producing a location of focus that detracts from the traditional church model. From a sociological viewpoint, however, things are so radically different from the pre-industrial age that the ministry of the church needs to reflect this.[5] People now live in one place, work in another and take their leisure in another still; a single parish no longer contains for individuals all the experience of life.

2. Sector ministers have been seen by some as a threat to the primacy of residential or parochial ministry. Over the last two decades the number of people being ordained by the church has steadily fallen. The work of parish clergy is increasingly being stretched and such clergy are taking on more responsibility than their predecessors. In some rural areas a single priest can be placed in charge of up to a dozen parishes. Viewed in this light, sector ministers can easily be cast in the role of parasites on diocesan resources. Some ask if it is right to continue to fund and allocate clergy for chaplaincies whilst the parish system is creaking as it tries to fulfil its historic responsibilities.

3. Some parish or residential clergy may feel that chaplains have opted out from the 'real' (and hard) work of parish ministry. Sector ministers, often unencumbered by work such as struggling to maintain costly mediaeval

buildings, can be characterized by some as inhabiting a cosseted, unreal world. Chaplains, and others, have pointed out that wherever human life is to be found, that is the real world. The institutions within which chaplaincies operate contain a variety of different human experience and life; they are communities in a very real sense and it is appropriate that the church exercises a ministry here as much as anywhere else.

4. Another factor that has prevented there being a better understanding between chaplains and parish clergy is the fact that chaplains almost invariably return, after some years in this sector ministry, to the parochial system. It is easy therefore for chaplaincy to be seen as an interruption, or a break from the real work of parish ministry. Unlike in other countries, most notably the Episcopal Church in the USA, in the United Kingdom chaplaincy is often not regarded as a long-term ministry.

This book is divided into three parts. Part One paints a background against which the individual chaplaincies can be set. In the opening chapter, Paul Avis challenges us to take seriously the context within which ministry takes place. After navigating us through the potential minefield of the churches' various attitudes to mission and ministry, Avis articulates a theology of ministry which sees sector ministry of fundamental importance because 'the church's mission is seriously weakened where it is channelled exclusively through territorial structures'. In the following chapter Christopher Moody, like Avis currently in parochial ministry (though having previously worked in chaplaincy), offers some metaphors which might be pertinent for sector ministry, in that they stimulate vision and point to the spiritual resources which exist in the world chaplaincy inhabits. In the third chapter of Part One, Sophie Gilliat-Ray places the establishment, growth and practice of sector ministry in a sociological context, charting the geographical and religious trends which have defined how much of chaplaincy has had to operate appropriately.

Part Two examines, in alphabetical order, individual sector ministries. Though by no means an exhaustive list of chaplaincies (space prevents it from being so), the chapters which make up the second part of the book look at the histories of the chaplaincies in various sectors and give reflections on the experiences of ordained ministry within these contexts.

In Part Three, Keith Lamdin considers the professional issues which arise from the experience of sector ministry. Lamdin looks at the development of 'good practice' in chaplaincy, how chaplains make sense of their experience as sector ministers and how this experience is related to the wider church. In the following chaper, anthropologist Gerald Arbuckle writes of the exciting possibilities for sector ministers to refound pastoral care and how chaplains are in a position to lead the churches in undertaking this task ecumenically. In a passage of biblical exegesis Arbuckle writes of how chaplains might see themselves as liminal persons, betwixt and between in terms of status and role. In the final chapter of the book James Woodward brings together all that has gone before. The chapter maps out how, through faithful presence, ministry and mission cannot be separated and questions some of the theological and practical assumptions made by some of the contributions which make up Part Two. As an open-ended piece of reflection it both asks how chaplains make sense of the context in which they operate and challenges those working in such sectors, whether ordained or not, to present sector ministries as a rightful part of the *mainstream* church.

The authors of the chapters of this book come from a wide variety of backgrounds. Because historically the Church of England has had the largest number of clergy working in sector ministry, the ecclesial allegiance of most authors reflects this fact, yet some contributors write from Roman Catholic and Free Church positions. Neither too are they exclusively English, nor indeed British. Whilst the experience shared here is mostly British, it is hoped that the histories and reflections of the ministries examined will be of a wider interest and use than for the British Isles alone. The issue of gender could have caused problems, with individuals being referred to as s/he or her/him, which made for clumsy reading. To simplify matters, gender has been alternated chapter by chapter.

Finally, I should like to thank a number of people who have been of help in bringing this book about. Ian Dickson, Elizabeth Bradley, Melanie Phillips and Robert Mitchell have given background information, time and other assistance, and meetings with university chaplaincy colleagues in London have given me much help. James Woodward gave valuable advice in helping outline the shape and content of the book and Leslie Houlden's friendship and encouragement I value immensely in personal terms and in offering an example of faithful and inspirational ministry. I am also extremely grateful to Bryan Blatch of the Royal Free Hospital School of Medicine, Diana Sanders of University College London Medical School and Alan Smith of the Royal Veterinary College for their support both of the post I occupy and of me personally. In producing this book, however, my greatest thanks are due to Ian Markham who, on one memorable holiday, whilst others were left fretting, helped prove the adage *solvitur ambulando*.

Giles Legood

Notes

1   For introductions to such ministries see Rod Hacking, *On the Boundary: A Vision for Non-stipendiary Ministry* (Norwich: Canterbury Press, 1990), and John Fuller and Patrick Vaughan (eds), *Working for the Kingdom: The Story of Ministers in Secular Employment* (London: SPCK, 1986).

2 An eminently readable account of contemporary ordained ministry within the Church of England is Robin Greenwood, *Transforming Priesthood: A New Theology of Mission and Ministry* (London: SPCK, 1994), which interestingly makes no mention of sector ministry.

3 This term was still being used in the 1970s; see, for instance, *Specialised Ministries* (London: Church Information Office, 1971).

4 National Society Working Party, *Sector Ministries* (London: National Society, 1983), p. 16.

5 For a sustained examination of this thesis see Grace Davie, *Religion in Britain Since 1945* (Oxford: Blackwell, 1994).

In memory of
Joan and Bob
Greta and Les

PART ONE

The context

1

Towards a theology of sector ministry

Paul Avis

A basic theology of ordained ministry cannot be one for which sector ministry constitutes the exception that proves the rule, but one that makes sense for sector ministry just as much as for parish-based or congregation-based ministries. Our purpose here therefore suggests a view of ministry that is not specific to certain contexts, either the parochial/congregational context or the context of the diverse institutions within which sector ministries are carried out, but is built on the essential mission of the Christian church wherever it operates. Let me try to illustrate the difference that context makes to ministry.

Ministry in its context

To start with, in parochial ministry the occasional offices loom large and present a significant challenge to our pastoral skills. Much of a parish priest's time and pastoral contact with individuals is concerned with preparing for and performing baptisms, marriages and funerals. By definition, therefore, a parish priest relates primarily to families of one sort or another (not necessarily the conventional middle-class nuclear family). A sector minister, on the other hand, relates much more to individuals, largely removed from the context and background provided by the family and the community. Again, a parish priest is often rather preoccupied with fund-raising – with leading and motivating the efforts of the parish to pay its parochial share to the diocese (or equivalent body in the Free churches) and to keep the fabric of its (parish) church in good repair (to take the two most pressing aspects of fund-raising). Sector ministry, in contrast, is usually comparatively free of the burden of fund-raising, since the worshipping community usually has its building (assuming it has one) provided by the organization within which it serves and is not required to pay parochial share – even when the stipend of the sector minister is wholly or partly met by the diocese or its equivalent. To take a final example, parish ministers and their equivalents in non-Anglican churches are often conscious of being on the sharp end of their church's line management: they are under the pastoral oversight and even canonical discipline of Rural Dean, Archdeacon and Bishop or their equivalents. The sector minister, in contrast, is relatively independent of the line management of the institutional church, though there may well be a senior chaplain, governing body, principal or head of the institution to whom they are accountable.

The differences of context and style between parochial or congregational ministers, on the one hand, and those in sector ministry, on the other, is such that it will not do simply to paint a portrait of what the ordained ministry does. What is called for is a theology, at least in simple outline, of the mission of the church and the part that the church's ordained ministers play in carrying this out. So I will venture a definition of the church's mission – its fundamental, God-given purpose.[1]

Mission and ministry

The Church's mission means the whole church bringing the whole Christ to the whole world. Let us look at this definition a little more closely.

- *The whole church.* Who or what is the subject of mission? In this holistic concept of mission, mission is the cutting edge of the total life of the church – a life of prayer, worship, confession of faith, teaching and preaching, baptizing, celebrating the Eucharist, providing a ministry of pastoral oversight, enjoying fellowship, bearing one another's burdens, bringing prophetic critique to bear on unjust and oppressive structures – and is carried out by all its members, lay and ordained.
- *The whole Christ.* What is the whole church communicating, promoting or offering? It is communicating the love of Christ to the suffering through compassionate service. It is the whole church, laity and clergy, bringing the whole Christ, embodied in the life of the church through all the means of grace, into effective engagement with human need.
- *The whole world.* Who or what is the object of this mission? It is to the whole world, that is to say, human life in all its fullness and diversity, manifested in all kinds of people, without regard to differences of race, culture, language, age or sex.

This holistic definition of mission is not merely a piece of rhetoric. It is grounded in a vital theological truth. It is actually called for because *our entire Christian existence is inherently missionary*. The missionary dynamic of Christian existence is orientated to a fundamental purpose of love flowing from the salvific will of God. The Second Vatican Council (1962–65), in laying down the doctrinal principles of the missionary activity of the Church, affirmed that 'the pilgrim Church is missionary by her very nature. For it is from the mission of the Son and the mission of the Holy Spirit that she takes her origin, in accordance with the decree of God the Father.'[2] This *missio Dei* is the overflowing of the love of God.

The Second Vatican Council goes on to insist that God's loving purpose for God's human creatures cannot be achieved in a purely individualistic or private way but only corporately and publicly, through the body or society of people ordained by God, namely the church, the new Israel. This structured community, the Council continues, has been endowed with the means of grace, principally word and sacrament, to bring about the participation of humankind in the transforming life that flows from God. The purpose of the church, therefore, is to bring to bear on the life of individuals and communities the salvific means of grace ordained and provided by God. 'The mission of the church, therefore, is fulfilled by that activity which makes her fully present to men and nations . . . Thus, by the example of her life and by her preaching, by the sacraments and other means of grace, she can lead them to the faith, the freedom and the peace of Christ.'[3]

Some of us, however, will already be asking, Where does evangelism come into this? What is the connection between mission and evangelism? The answer must be that there is a connection – an absolutely vital one – but not an equivalence. If mission is the cutting edge of the whole life of the church, it is nevertheless not identical with evangelism. Evangelism (or evangelization) is the part of which mission is the whole. Evangelism is, as Bosch defines it, 'the proclamation of salvation in Christ to those who do not believe in him, calling them to repentance and conversion, announcing forgiveness of sin, and inviting them to become living members of Christ's earthly community and to begin a life of service to others in the power of the Holy Spirit'.[4] Or as Moltmann puts it: 'Evangelisation is mission, but mission is not merely evangelisation.'[5] What is implicit in mission becomes explicit in evangelism. God's gracious will for the wholeness and healing of human life entails a commitment by Christians and churches to work for greater social, political and economic well-being as well as to proclaim the gospel in word and sacrament. Evangelism brings into sharper focus what the church stands for at all times and in all its activities and is therefore an essential component of mission. As the Archbishop of Canterbury has insisted: 'Mission which does not have evangelism as a focus is not Christian mission; and evangelism which keeps itself aloof from matters of justice and human welfare does not reflect adequately the biblical revelation.'[6] Mission and evangelism are thus integrally related and grounded in the same theological principle that the church carries out its God-given task by doing the things that it has been commissioned to do. What precisely is this commission? If it cannot be identified with evangelism, without remainder, what is the task of the church?

My answer is that the task or purpose (mission) of the church takes the form of a *ministry*, that is to say, a form of service. The mission or fundamental task of the church is to carry out a ministry of word, sacrament and pastoral care. In the Great Commission of Matthew 28:19–20 these are unambiguously present. We hear of three activities: teaching (word), baptism (sacrament) and fostering discipleship (pastoral care). 'Go therefore to all nations and make them my disciples; baptise them in the name of the Father and the Son and the Holy Spirit, and teach them to observe all that I have commanded you.' The threefold task of ministering word, sacrament and pastoral care corresponds to the threefold mission of Jesus Christ as prophet (word), priest (sacrament) and king (pastoral care). It also corresponds to the threefold vocation given to bishops, priests, deacons and laity as set out so clearly in the documents of Vatican II: teaching, sanctifying and governing (or leading).[7] The work of teaching ministers the word; the work of sanctifying ministers the sacraments; and the work of governing ministers pastoral care and oversight. Mission, and within it evangelism, is the church being the church and living out the totality of its divinely grounded life.

The tasks of ministry

We need now to be clear about what we mean by ministry. I would define ministry as *work for the church that is recognized by the church*. Ministry occurs when a person, whether lay or ordained, performs a task on behalf of the community that is authorized or in some way recognized by the community. All Christians have received a charism of the Holy Spirit through baptism. Every limb or organ of the body of Christ has a vital role for the well-being of the whole body (1 Corinthians 12). All are called to minister and when their ministry is recognized and owned by the community they are seen to act in the name of Christ. Thus ministry is public and representative, rather than private and individual. As O'Meara has put it: 'Christian ministry is the public activity of a baptized follower of Jesus Christ flowing from the Spirit's charism and an individual personality on behalf of a Christian community to witness to, serve and realize the kingdom of God.'[8]

All ministry, whether ordained or lay, is – and can only be – the ministry of Jesus Christ in his church. Ministry is simply Christ at work through the presence of the Holy Spirit, teaching, sanctifying and governing his body through inadequate and unworthy human instruments. For example, Christ himself is the true minister of baptism, because baptism is an act of prevenient divine grace that unites the believer to Christ in his death and resurrection. Clearly only Christ can unite a person to himself. As Luther used to insist, it is Christ who splashes the water on your head. Similarly, the Eucharist is the sacrament of our continuing communion with Christ and with one another in the body of Christ. Christ gives his body and blood (i.e. himself, the whole Christ) by means of the elements of bread and wine. Because Christ gives himself to us in the Eucharist, uniting us in his self-oblation to the Father, he is the true minister of the Eucharist. When we receive, we receive Christ as though from Christ.

Christian ministry is ultimately the ministry of Jesus Christ because ministry is grounded in baptism, the foundational sacrament of the church, and it is through baptism that Christians are united with Christ in his death and resurrection and share in his threefold office as Prophet, Priest and King (1 Peter 2:5, 9; cf. *Lumen Gentium* 10, of Vatican II). As prophets, Christians discern and proclaim the word of God. As priests, they offer spiritual sacrifices of prayer, praise, gifts and ultimately themselves. As a *royal* priesthood, they play their part in the governance of Christ's kingdom. Baptism incorporates a believer into the ministerial community.

It follows from the significance of baptism, as our incorporation into a ministerial community, that all ministry is *representative* in that it consists of public actions, owned by the community, that manifest the nature and life of the community. The public ministers of the church represent both Christ and the church (or as we could say, Christ-in-the-church) – not in the vicarious sense that they take the place of an absent Christ, but in the realist sense that they make Christ truly present and show forth the true nature of the church as his body. The ministry leads the way in doing what the church must do and acting as the church must act. The authenticity of the church is concerned with its apostolicity. A broad ecumenical consensus defines the apostolic tradition of the church as 'continuity in the permanent characteristics of the church of the apostles: witness to the apostolic faith, proclamation and fresh interpretation of the gospel, celebration of baptism and the eucharist, the transmission of ministerial responsibilities, communion in prayer, love, joy and suffering, service to the sick and the needy, unity among the local churches and sharing the gifts which the Lord has given to each'.[9] When the church engages in the work that it has been called to do, it manifests its continuity with the mission and ministry of the apostles. When it is apostolic the church is simply being itself, fulfilling its nature.

The ministerial task of the church is fourfold: proclaiming the word, administering the sacraments, providing pastoral care and exercising conciliarity. Article XIX of the Church of England states the consensus of Reformation theology that the church is identified by the twin actions of preaching the word and administering the sacraments: 'The visible Church of Christ is a congregation of faithful men, in the which the pure Word of God is preached, and the Sacraments be duly ministered according to Christ's ordinance . . .'

This does not mention pastoral care or conciliarity, but they can be seen to be implied in the ministry of word and sacrament. Pastoral care is simply the extension and application of word and sacrament to individuals in their particular circumstances. Word and sacrament are not offered on a 'take it or leave it' basis, but are set in the context of pastoral support and guidance. Similarly, the ministry of conciliarity is required in order that word, sacrament and pastoral care may be provided in right and proper forms and that the church may act with integrity and consistency.

1. Proclaiming the word is a primary form of ministry. For the Reformers and now for Vatican II, the word of the gospel constitutes the church and brings it into being. As Vatican II says, echoing St Mark, Jesus Christ inaugurated the Christian church by preaching the gospel (Mark 1.14–15; *Lumen Gentium* 5). The ministry of the word includes proclaiming the gospel by every possible appropriate means and expounding the scriptures to provide instruction in the faith. To preach the gospel of Christ, which is the power of God unto salvation (Romans 1:16), is a – perhaps we should say *the* – primary task of the church. But along with proclamation (*kerygma*) goes instruction (*didache*) whereby the faithful are built up as the body of Christ (Ephesians 4:12). Both these tasks of the church are expressions of its apostolicity, for the church is apostolic when it is grounded in the apostolic proclamation and faithful to the apostolic mission. Among the multiplicity of permanent characteristics of the church of the apostles, both proclamation and instruction are signs of its apostolicity.

2. Celebrating the sacraments of the church is also a primary form of ministry. Among the principal means of grace to sustain Christians in the life of the church are the sacraments instituted by Jesus Christ according to the New Testament. Protestants and Anglicans understand these to be baptism and the Eucharist, while Roman Catholics and Eastern Orthodox have a longer list. But even the two dominical sacraments belong in a wider sacramental context. They find their place among all the recognized expressions of the sacramental principle, of sacramentality, involved in worship, ministry and mission. For wherever the word of God is joined to significant actions to comprise an outward visible sign of an inward spiritual reality the sacramental principle is at work.

   Other expressions of the sacramentality of the life of the church are grounded in the essential ecclesial tasks of preaching and teaching the faith and administering the sacraments. Thus Confirmation may be regarded as a pastoral application of the fundamental Christian initiation in baptism which, following further instruction in the faith and the personal acceptance of it, is expressed in a sacramental way through the sign of the laying on of the hands of the bishop and prayer for the confirmation of the Holy Spirit. Similarly, sacramental confession or penance may be requested by a penitent with a troubled conscience that is not assuaged by the general confession made in public worship. Here we have a further pastoral application of the gospel of salvation and of the one baptism for the remission of sins – in other words, a particular form of the ministry of word and sacrament. Anointing the sick (James 5:14–15), enacted in faith and in the name of the Lord, is a further pastoral application of the ministry of word and an outward sign to a particular circumstance. Again, prayer and praise in worship and the sanctifying of stages of life's journey in the occasional offices (the so-called rites of passage), such as marriage and funeral rites, are held within the framework of the ministry of word and sacrament in the context of pastoral care. These are all means of grace that sustain Christian people in the life-giving milieu of the body of Christ.

Baptism is the fundamental sacrament of initiation into the body of Christ and thus into the *koinonia* of the church. Baptism consists of the sacramental action with the element of water and the accompanying Trinitarian confession of faith – matter and form – for there can be no sacrament without the integral contribution of the word. Baptism constitutes the ultimate ground of all Christian ministry, whether lay or ordained, for all forms of ministry are none other than the ministry of Christ in his church. As the Anglican–Reformed dialogue put it: 'The primary ministry is that of the risen Christ himself, and we are enabled to participate in it by the power of the Spirit.'[10]

3. The pastoral ministry is another primary form of Christian ministry. There is an emerging ecumenical consensus that pastoral oversight *(episkope)* is necessary to the church. Pastoral ministry seems to fall into two categories. First, there is primary pastoral care, when prayerful support, comfort and guidance are offered to sick, bereaved or troubled individuals. Second, there is the more prescriptive ministry of oversight, advice, discipline and spiritual direction. In a voluntary society this can only be offered, not imposed. It can only be given to the extent that individuals are willing to accept it.

4. Finally, conciliarity belongs to the fourfold ministry or task of the church, though it is not always recognized as such. Conciliarity refers to the ministry of consultation, discernment and decision-making when the church comes together through representative and constitutional channels, such as synods and councils, to take counsel for its well-being and mission. Though synodical government is often disparaged, it is an

essential function of the church and brings to light the nature of the body of Christ as a community of laity and clergy, women and men, who have a common concern and shared responsibility for the whole.

Representative ministry

If ministry is work for the church that is authorized or acknowledged by the church, then it follows that representativeness is a principle that applies to all aspects of ministry. The church's ministers are called to represent Christ, to be his ambassadors (2 Corinthians 5:20), to speak and act in his name. There is only one mission – that of Jesus Christ through his body the church: laity and clergy share in the common task according to the gifts of the Holy Spirit in the church. But there is also, so to speak, an economy in the distribution of ministries and the authority to minister. The ancient Greek patristic concept of economy (*oikonomia*) implies that there is a God-given purpose governing and regulating the life of the church and that, in order to promote that purpose, there is a particular distribution of gifts, tasks, responsibilities and the authority to fulfil them. Economy suggests restraint, discipline and the various distribution of responsibilities – in other words, holy order. By virtue of holy order, a pattern of ministry is appointed in the Church. The Roman Catholic, Eastern Orthodox, Anglican, Old Catholic and some Lutheran churches adhere to the threefold ministry of bishops, priests and deacons, ordained in historical succession. The non-episcopal Protestant churches have their own distribution of representative ministries in which the principle of holy order is respected within a greater equality of ministries. Now let us see how the principle of divine economy applies to representativeness.

There is a vital sense in which all the baptized have a representative ministry. I take ministry, properly speaking, to be service offered to God in the church which is recognized by the church. It is not the purely personal witness that Christians bear to Christ, but has a public dimension. Recent theology of ministry (O'Meara, 1983; Collins, 1992)[11] has stressed that there is an element of commissioning and therefore of authority in all ministry. Because ministry manifests Christ, the Servant King, it embodies both authority and the spirit of service. Ministry is a task carried out on behalf of the body which is recognized by the body. There is, of course, a private and individual aspect to this. Through faith and baptism Christians are united with Christ. Their Christ-centred identity means that all Christians, when living out their calling, represent Christ to others. All represent Christ and his church by virtue of their baptism which has united them to Christ in his death and resurrection. All the baptized are *in persona Christi*. They carry Christ in their hearts and witness to him in their lives. The momentum of Christian spirituality and mission stems from the fact that the baptized live, speak and act for Christ. They are individually members of his body and temples of the Holy Spirit (1 Corinthians 6:19).

But we are concerned primarily with the public and representative aspect of ministry. The principle of representativeness is seen, I suggest, particularly clearly in the ministry of the ordained, for within the body of Christ there are ministries that are given authority to speak and act in a public way that goes beyond what lay people are authorized to do. The ordained are called, trained, commissioned, licensed and accountable to authority in a particular way. Through the ministry of word and sacrament and the exercise of pastoral oversight they carry out a public ministry of Christ. Though all the baptized share in Christ's threefold messianic office of prophet, priest and king, individuals may not take it upon themselves to claim a public ministry for themselves in which they speak and act on behalf of all. As Luther insisted, what is given to the whole body no private individual may arrogate to themselves without the authority of the body. Similarly, the Thirty-nine Articles state: 'It is not lawful for any man to take upon him the office of publick preaching, or ministering the Sacraments in the Congregation, before he be lawfully called, and sent to execute the same . . . by men who have publick authority given unto them' (Article XXIII).

The Anglican–Reformed dialogue states: 'The minister as leader has a representative character, to act as "the one on behalf of the many", so that the whole Church is represented in his person as he carries on his heart the concerns of all his people. He does not act in his own name, but in the name of Christ, and in the name of the whole body of Christ, so that he is at once the mouthpiece of our Lord and the mouthpiece of his flock.'[12]

The Priesthood of the Ordained Ministry says: 'The ordained ministry has a representative function, both in relation to Christ and in relation to the whole community of faith. It has a particular relationship to Christ, which is not simply derived from the common ministry of all Christians, both in representing Christ to his people and also, in union with him, in representing the people to the Father.' The report goes on to say: 'Bishops and presbyters represent both Christ and his people in their leadership of the Church and its mission, in the proclamation of the Gospel, in the articulation of faith, and in the celebration of the sacraments.'[13]

It is these ministries, carried out with the authority that Christ bestows through the church in the threefold order, rather than the private person of bishops, priests and deacons, that effectively represent Christ to the church and the world. It is not that the person of the ordained minister as a private individual represents Christ but that Christ is present in the appointed means of grace ministered by that person with the authority and charism bestowed in ordination. The only ministry of the church – of laity and clergy – is the ministry of Jesus Christ himself. That is why the church insists that the unworthiness of the minister does not destroy the efficacy of the means of grace (Article XXVI). But within the economy of holy order there are various callings through which Christ ministers to his body and through his body to the world. The principle of representativeness, properly understood and safeguarded, is vital because it insists that the risen Christ works through unworthy human instruments to minister his grace and presence for the salvation of the world. With the authority that comes from Christ-in-his-body, these appointed ministries of word, sacrament and pastoral oversight re-present Christ in ways that he has ordained within the economy of the one *missio Dei*.

Sector ministers and representativeness

In conclusion, we must consider the specific way in which sector ministry can represent Christ-in-his-church and so carry forward the mission or ministry that Christ has given to the church. The way in which sector ministry can do this is a function of the diverse forms of community in which it ministers.

In his study of secularization, Alan Gilbert argued that 'churches as social organisations are effective only when their own structures mirror those of the societies which they seek to serve'. 'In order to thrive', he continued, 'they must adapt themselves to the basic social divisions and settlement patterns of their constituencies.' The mediaeval parochial system, where church and community structures were coterminous, provided an obvious example of the ideal relationship between church and community.[14] The church is predisposed to mirror, in its own organization, the established contours of social identity.

However, the progressive urbanization of Britain during the past two hundred years, to the point where 90 per cent of the population lives in cities and towns, has created an environment that is not generally supportive of traditional models of religious community. Geographical mobility creates rootlessness, damages community identity, disperses families and undermines loyalty to place. The social identity of the urban dweller is only minimally territorial. This obviously weakens the appeal of the churches and the purchase they have on the population, since they remain primarily territorial in organization and ethos. Gilbert, writing nearly twenty years ago, castigated the churches for failing to adapt to the new situation:

> Organised religion, everywhere in the British Isles, has failed to cope with the decline of the territorial community and the emergence of pluralistic, partial communities. The idea of territory remains central to Christian planning, both pastoral and evangelistic, and church leaders still tend to

think of work among newer, functional communities as 'special ministries' . . . a 'real' church must have some territorial identity.[15]

The church's mission is seriously weakened where it is channelled exclusively through territorial structures. Organizational and institutional structures offer an alternative milieu for mission. The imperative of mission suggests, therefore, that where opportunities for chaplaincies or sector ministries are available, they should be seized with both hands. Where institutions are unwilling to fund sector ministries wholly, such ministries should be funded by the church as a priority, even at the expense of parochial ministry. Dioceses need a strong parochial power base in order to fund missionary outreach through sector ministries. Developing patterns of collaborative ministry, where lay people and clergy work together in benefice-wide ministry teams, so reducing the dependence on dwindling supplies of stipendiary clergy, should eventually help to make more funding available for this purpose. In many situations, in institutions and organizations, it is Christian lay people who must bear the brunt of witness and ministry: they need to be increasingly equipped and motivated for this. However, there will always be a need for those who are regarded in the community as the church's 'official representatives', the ordained ministers, who have the calling, training and commissioning to minister word, sacrament and pastoral care in the name of Christ's church and who are the publicly identifiable agents of the church's mission. Their presence is needed increasingly beyond the parochial, territorial framework in precisely those contexts where people are educated, nursed and healed, restrained and disciplined, enjoy their leisure activities and do a specialized job of work. That, just as much as the parochial/congregational context, is the mission field of today.

It remains vital, however, for sector ministers to see themselves as part of that overall mission – a mission that the church carries out by means of various ministries. It is not difficult for parish/congregational ministers to see themselves as the agents of a mission that is given to the church as a body – as a structured society, ordained by God, with means of grace that are regulated by appropriate authority. However, even among parochial/congregational ministers there is significant alienation from the church's structures of oversight and a tendency to regard the synodical (conciliar) work of the church and even the ministry of the bishop as almost irrelevant to the 'real' work of the church at the grass roots. Such congregationalist attitudes are to be deplored as profoundly uncatholic.

But how much more difficult must it be for sector ministers, who may be working in comparative isolation from ordained colleagues and from systems of support and oversight, to retain a sense of belonging to the whole. I imagine that there can be a temptation to drift away from that fundamental sense, articulated so clearly in the ecclesiology of Vatican II, that the mission of the church is given to an ordered, structured, visible society that has the God-given authority to oversee the forms and channels by which God's saving grace is ministered to the world through word, sacrament and pastoral care. Sector ministers should never have to feel that they are forgotten, overlooked or neglected by the church that has called, trained, ordained and licensed them. But on the other hand, their comparatively relaxed relationship to diocesan or other structures of oversight and accountability should not tempt them to act as though they were unaccountable freelance ministers rather than part of the body or college of the ordained within the ordered society that is the church. Sector ministers should be affirmed as an integral part of the mission and ministry of the Christian church.

Notes

1   See further Paul Avis, *Mission after Modernity* (London: forthcoming), ch. 1.
2   W. M. Abbott (ed.), *The Documents of Vatican II* (London: Geoffrey Chapman, 1966) p. 585.
3   Ibid., pp. 589–90.
4   D. Bosch, *Transforming Mission* (Maryknoll, New York: Orbis, 1992), pp. 10–11.
5   Quoted ibid., pp. 411–12.
6   G. Carey, *The Way Ahead: Preparing the Church of England for the New Millennium* (The Ashe Lecture: private circulation, 1997), p. 7.
7   See K. B. Osborne, *Priesthood in the Roman Catholic Church* (New York: Paulist, 1988), pp. 307–42.
8   T. F. O'Meara, *Theology of Ministry* (New York: Paulist, 1983), p. 142.
9   Faith and Order Commission, *Baptism, Eucharist and Ministry* (Geneva: WCC, 1982), M34.
10 Anglican–Reformed International Commission, *God's Reign and Our Unity* (London: SPCK, 1984), no. 74.
11 See O'Meara, op. cit., and J. N. Collins, *Are All Christians Ministers?* (Newtown NSW/Brunswick, Victoria: E. J. Dwyer/David Lovell, 1992).
12 *God's Reign and Our Unity*, op. cit., no. 85.
13 Board for Mission and Unity, *The Priesthood of the Ordained Ministry* (London: Church House Publishing, 1986), no. 144.
14 A. Gilbert, *The Making of Post-Christian Britain* (London and New York: Longmans, 1980), p. 80.
15 Ibid., pp. 84–5.

2

Spirituality and sector ministry

Christopher Moody

Half-way up the hill from the small port to the high town in Patmos is the cave where St John the Apostle is supposed to have had the visions which form the Book of Revelation. At the top of the hill is the monastery of St John, founded at a later date by another saint, a heavily protected enclosure that admits tourists and pilgrims very much on its own terms. Down below, the actual business of tourism, on which the whole island largely depends, goes on day and night. It has always intrigued me that the most holy place on Patmos, the cave where St John had his visions, seems less important than the monastery at the top of the hill, when it is actually more important. It is both some way off the beaten track *and* the place of vision.

The cave on Patmos seems to be a metaphor with many possible applications. It is certainly a good metaphor for the position sector ministers often feel they are in, caught between the demands of the institutional church somewhere above their heads and the call to be alongside others 'down below' in the actual business of a secular organization. The temptation for the sector minister is always to find a more secure place to be, to 'fit in', either by acting as a professional among other professionals and speaking their language, or by creating a highly fenced enclosure for fellow religionists. It is good to be reminded that, though we often feel trapped between two worlds that belong properly to others, and marginal to both, it is the place 'in the fields of charity and sin / where we shall lead our harvest in'.

It is also a place of vision. It is often only those who stand on the margins who see the wider picture and who stand for 'the something more' that is there to be discovered in any situation, good or bad. The special charism we need in sector ministry is the ability to hold that position, conforming to neither reality 'above' or 'below' us, wanting neither to return to the safety of our religious denomination, nor to belong anywhere else. This chapter suggests some of the metaphors one might use to organize the experience of this ministry in a way that stimulates vision and points to the spiritual resources that exist amid the often messy, tense and garbled dealings we have with those whose world we share.

A wilderness ministry

One of the attractions of sector ministry is that it brings you closer to the pressures of people's workaday world. You have left the security embraced by the term 'church life' and gone down the hill to the level of ordinary human experience. Here you are acting on other people's territory rather than your own and any space you might create for 'God-talk' is something that has to be negotiated – a missionary principle which the secure boundaries of parish ministry still allow many priests to ignore. When you meet people in the parochial context, it is often when they have had time, either as they enter church or as you enter their home, to organize their responses and put on a good front. You may know of the pressures that people suffer from work or family relationships but often it is at second hand. As a chaplain, on the other hand, you are often in the position of *participant observer*, subject to some of the same pressures from the institution as its other members, and able to observe situations as they occur. You are able, therefore, to enter into the wilderness of people's daily experience in a way that the occasions for meeting characteristic of parish ministry often prevent.

Working alongside others as a member of an institution to which you also 'belong', albeit not in the same way as others, means that you can communicate with individuals more easily on the level of half-articulated and unorganized religious thought and feeling, without the usual caution and embarrassment. Often you do not know quite how to handle and interpret what is being shared. This again is part of the wilderness experience, finding your way by spiritual intuition and insight, without the usual flags and signposts. The proximity to actual events, albeit within a closed environment such as a prison, a hospital or an army base, makes you much more consciously aware of the overwhelming nature of people's daily experience. Professor David Ford has typified modern experience as one of 'multiple overwhelmings' induced by the immediate pressures on individual lives of insecurity in employment and in core relationships, and by the wider anxiety evoked by consistent and rapid change in both their local context and the world as a whole. This is focused in many institutions by the constant restructuring and changes in direction that put the pressure on individuals to succeed in achieving new goals for the institution, whilst simultaneously discounting their previous experience. The sector minister is able to enter the wilderness of that experience and that changes the character of the pastoral relationship.

This quality of 'being in the wilderness' is reinforced in many institutional contexts by the fact that students, patients, prisoners or new recruits have been cut adrift from the normal ties which secure their sense of identity and self worth and feel lost and confused. So, ironically, in many situations, managers and other professionals who experience themselves as 'overwhelmed' in one way are ministering to and directing people who are being 'overwhelmed' in another. The potential for disaster is always present. Recent research in the United States suggests that the workplace is where people increasingly look for the satisfaction of their personal need for friendship and belonging as well as for professional achievement and financial gain. They often have all their eggs in one basket. This makes the threat posed by constant change and restructuring all the more dangerous. The highest hopes compete with the deepest despair and cynicism. And yet, precisely because it is a dangerous and highly insecure place to be emotionally, people can emerge from such experiences, having reached the limits of their known capacities and competence, totally transformed. Like Elijah in the wilderness, brought to the point of exhaustion by his own efforts and the enmity of the powers that be, it is in the midst of such turmoil we discover the 'still small voice' which simultaneously reassures us and renews our sense of purpose (1 Kings 19:1–18).

Jesus, in his parable, describes the wilderness as a place where unclean spirits roam about seeking rest (Matthew 12:43–45). The whole field of work and the professions is highly charged with energy. It is the place where we can directly experience the high satisfaction derived from constructive engagement with some aspect of reality and, at the same time, the shadow side of manipulation, naked power and disorganization. It is not surprising that many sector ministers, though they are often at the limit of their own resources and at a loss, find it hard, after experiencing this highly charged atmosphere, to return to local, parochial ministry. As, in biblical tradition, the wilderness was the place where demonic energy was unleashed and unmasked, so, paradoxically, it could become the place where God, also, would make himself known directly within the context of spiritual conflict and encounter. Thus, to minister in such a context is to be made aware of how far we are acted upon all the time by forces beyond our control, but also how we are able to seize the initiative to intervene at a crucial stage in the life journeys of others. It is often a peripatetic and anonymous ministry, undertaken without demonstrable results in terms of one's congregation or reputation, but deeply satisfying. To work in a secular institution in which there is a high turnover in staff and personnel and the ability for long-term planning is severely restricted, is to be made aware of the sacrament of the present moment and what it requires of us in terms of a different sort of preparedness. We simply do not know where many of the relationships we establish with individuals are leading, but the potential for disclosure and life-changing encounter is always there. However, this space for encounter is always being threatened, both by the institution's desire to see measurable results and by our own lack of humility and patience. It requires a particular kind of spirituality to be able to loiter on the edge of other people's lives, to be fully engaged and yet watchful at the same time. Above all, it requires a sense of Christ's spiritual presence in every aspect of human activity and struggle – a presence that can be chanced upon at any moment in the cell, or consulting room, at the bar or in a hospital corridor.

There is another sense, also, in which the sector minister works in a wilderness, which has more to do with language. I read recently that in a medieval map only discovered this century, a Franciscan missionary had systematically crossed out the remarks 'here be dragons' and 'here be demons' with which the cartographers had signalled the limits of their knowledge, and substituted 'here be God'. The sector minister often works in that uncharted area between clearly identified religious roles and language, informed by his own faith, training and denominational allegiance, and the purely pragmatic concern of the institution and its leaders to ensure it runs smoothly and survives. He often feels called upon to think about and address questions about the ethos and the moral dilemmas and ambiguities underlying an institution's purposes. It is not easy in such circumstances to know when religious language is being used merely to cloak an institution's secular purposes and protect its ideological base, or, on the other hand, when spiritual realities are being touched on in the purely secular language people within the institution use about its life.

The ministry of in between

It should be clear from what I have written already that I believe that the primary datum with which the minister works is that provided by the context itself, not one imported by the minister from outside. This means learning the language of the institution to which one belongs, both the formal language of its procedures, memos and mission statements and the informal language used about it in canteens and common rooms. It means trying to discover what the ethos of the institution is and the various ways in which it finds expression. It means 'unlearning' many of the categories provided by one's previous experience and theological training and catching hold of the arbitrary, non-specific language of 'unchurched' religious experience. We have to be, in Robert J. Schreiter's phrase, 'local theologians' capable of understanding the different histories contained within an institution and the ways in which they can be read. This means not falling automatically for the official version, being aware of the ambiguities of people's experience and the dimly understood ways in which questions of faith and value are often expressed. But this is not to leave the experience of the institution and the people within it where it is, unquestioned and uninterpreted by contact with the wider stream of religious tradition of which the church in all its manifestations is the guardian. In fact that is precisely what people require of us; in particular, finding informal liturgies of various sorts that express the truth of their situation but still have the authority conferred by contact with the universal symbols of the Christian faith.

To this purpose, it is important that we remain religious 'outsiders' in whatever context we find ourselves. Every institution has the tendency to provide total explanations for people's behaviour in terms of its own institutional aims and ideals. Patients, prisoners and students are given the label 'difficult' on the basis of how well they fit the roles assigned to them by the institution. I am aware when I use the word 'institution' that I am using a convenient shorthand for the complex means by which a necessary hierarchy of leadership, authority and decision-making is maintained within a given field of human endeavour. I am not, therefore, using the term pejoratively. It remains true, however, that in any institution, definitions are made, roles are assigned, and some people have less power than others to control these. The definitions may have nothing to do with a person's actual behaviour. For example, a prisoner may be violent to himself or others but not considered 'difficult' because he falls within the usual categories for what is considered normal behaviour ('Once you know how to handle him, he's all right'). A chaplain has the power to challenge some of these definitions precisely because of his amphibious nature as someone acting outside the usual constraints of his own institution – the church in its denominational form – but not conforming totally to the constraints of the other in which he is placed. This is valuable for the chaplains themselves, the people they are working with and even the institution itself. Sector ministers should always be careful of abandoning this position for something better defined and more 'useful' in the institution's terms, for example, becoming a student counsellor, or being accepted as a member of the psychiatric team in a mental hospital. They have the ability, if they negotiate their role well, to point to the 'something more' in any situation. This freedom can only come from their position as privileged outsiders, faithful to their own spiritual discipline, and not therefore to all the norms of the institution in which they work. Individuals within the institution often initiate conversations on the basis of the perceived difference between the two. The sector minister may be the one person individuals feel they can confide in without compromising their academic or professional future or their standing among their peers.

This position is privileged in one sense but precarious in another. We are people with 'statusless status', given a crucial role to play in particular situations but ignored much of the time. Where do we find the spiritual resources to fulfil such a role when we are deprived of so much of the social reinforcement which usually accompanies the priestly or pastoral role in denominational church life? That is the most crucial question, daunting but exciting at the same time. How do we discover the springs of a spirituality that is responsive to the needs and challenges of the environment we are in, but constantly and deeply refreshed by resources beyond it? How do we find a language that shares some of the central concerns and preoccupations people have within their workaday environment but encourages reflection, freedom and a deeper level of concern (and detachment) at the same time? The rest of this chapter points up some of the metaphors for this elusive ministry mediating between one level of reality and another. The only thing these metaphors have in common is that they are all non-institutional and non-professional descriptions. Given the distance from their own sources of professional identity in which most sector ministers work, this makes them specially relevant.

Shamans

The first description is the most controversial. Shamans are traditionally the people that bona fide religious representatives struggle *against* – chancers and charlatans, the purveyors of myth and magic rather than serious truth. The modern shaman usually draws his title and his inspiration from some 'New Age' philosophy rather than orthodox Christianity. Nevertheless, it is a useful term for a number of reasons.

First of all, it points to the marginal nature of many people's experience of 'God' in our society. The Enlightenment attacked the notion of God as a God of the gaps – whatever was left without explanation after the process of scientific experiment and enquiry had been completed. What we are left with nowadays, when there is so much more pessimism about 'explanations' of all kinds, is a God of the 'cracks' – those elements of semi-mystical experience which are not open to explanation at all. God has been pushed to the margins of ordinary experience – to the moments of crisis, healing, ecstasy or union which are normally hidden by ordinary life. Beneath the apparent secularism of our society is 'a riotous unreason at least as virulent as the crass scientism which dismisses all signals of transcendence as mere superstition on a par with the tooth fairy'.[1] Because of his distance from the ecclesiastical institution, this level of religiosity forms the point of departure for many of the sector minister's contacts with others. We cannot begin a conversation by discounting this level of experience altogether. Whether we include or exclude it, eventually, we have to treat it seriously.

This is reinforced, secondly, by the fact that in the educational and caring institutions in which many sector ministers work, where 'the effective exploitation or control of the self is at a premium' among the carers, there is a corresponding focus upon personal meaning, autonomy and self-healing. A religious approach based on the denial of such concerns, in favour of the notion of inherited guilt, sin and an absolute morality, for instance, is unlikely to get very far in these circumstances. 'It is in these social sectors that the fragility of institutions and the uncertainties of the homeless self are most keenly experienced',[2] especially in a period of rapid change and restructuring. This has to be taken seriously as the focus of any spiritual quest alongside others. Many people will be more interested in religious belief and practice as a largely self-administered therapy, rather than a system of explanation. What they will be seeking from the sector minister will be evidence of genuine spiritual experience rather than well-worked-out arguments. The phrase I used earlier – 'statusless status' – is actually a term used by Victor Turner to describe an African shaman's status as a healer in a dominant group that is not his own. This is often the only status sector ministers enjoy within secular institutions. To act as a minister is such a situation is to accept that one must work, for the most part, at the level of shared personal experience and with whatever projections – magical or otherwise – a point of contact is initiated.

Watchers

As outsiders, given a privileged position often, but with little or no influence, sector ministers are often in the position of onlookers. This can induce a feeling of guilt or powerlessness as we watch what is happening, able to sympathize individually, but not to determine particular outcomes. The temptation is to avoid such a position by business of various kinds – either building up a list of clients or a chapel congregation, serving on committees or finding an issue which gives one a more definite public profile. These may be good in themselves but not if they prevent a wider engagement with the life of the institution. The one thing we may be endowed with that other people do not have is time. There has to be a contemplative side to our ministry in the sense of a willed passivity which relinquishes constant activity in favour of a wider apprehension of what is going on, and which uncovers the deeper implications of apparently small events, chance remarks and encounters. It is the only way in which we can build up the quality of attention and preparedness that allows us to seize the opportunities for ministry when they arise. It is the opposite of daydreaming in that it is focused on the task in hand and cannot be maintained without a strong sense of purpose and priorities. 'Seek ye first the kingdom of God and his righteousness [i.e. rather than the sort of activity which is self-promoting and self-justifying] and all these things shall be added unto you' (Matthew 6:33). It is more analogous to the creative reverie which precedes and accompanies the making of a painting or a poem or the survey of scientific data in pursuit of a theorem. Often it will be troubling rather than satisfying. It exposes one directly to the flux, pain and costly human effort at the heart of so much institutional life, the intractability of so many of its problems, the individual selfishness and abuse of authority, the general sense of cynicism or apathy that wastes or deflects so much energy. Often it will end in no immediate result in terms of a bright idea or project. But without this willingness to enter the 'travail' of whatever is going on, there can be no real act of discernment or vision. The fruits of such reflection may emerge only later on, as they did in Jesus' repeated instruction to his disciples to 'watch and pray' as they approached the events of his passion.

I hesitated between the word 'watcher' and the word 'prophet' to describe this aspect of sector ministry. The two are closely connected. The prophets, after all, were called the watchmen of Israel. But I settled in the end for 'watcher'. The term 'prophetic ministry' has been used a little too glibly in relation to sector ministry. It sometimes masks the absence of any ongoing role within the secular context or in relationship to the church as a whole. It seems too much like an excuse to cover up our anxiety about that. That anxiety seems to me, on the other hand, to be something we should do our best to *embrace* in any spirituality of sector ministry. The anonymity of so much chaplaincy work is part of its special charism. The sector minister works very much from the periphery inwards rather than the centre outwards, and that means accepting that much of one's best work will be largely overlooked. However, there are three ways in particular that a chaplain's 'watchfulness' may result in him fulfilling a prophetic service either to individuals or to the institution. Firstly, he can seize the opportunity with individuals at critical moments in their lives, acting as a midwife for a life-changing decision, the birth of a vocation, or the resolution to some inner threat or turmoil. Secondly, he can initiate particular activities that supply some lack or deficit in an institution's life, for example, the kind and degree of care for the dying and bereaved in hospital, or which point beyond its immediate concerns to the wider community. And thirdly, he can challenge and unmask the illegitimate claims and burdens an institution places on the time, loyalty, personal morality and beliefs of its individual members. Every institution has the tendency to provide total explanations for its own purposes that exclude other points of view and sources of critique. In that sense, all institutions are naturally idolatrous. For that very same reason, our loyalty to a religious tradition beyond the life of a particular institution is the greatest service we can provide for it. However, if we are either too narrowly sectarian or too uncritically affirmative of its life, we lose our position as a watcher who can help an institution check and revision its life in the light of its contribution to a greater whole.

Resident aliens

If I had to find one source alone in the biblical narrative of metaphors for sector ministry, it would be in the wanderings of the patriarchs in Genesis, people who were dwelling already within the land of promise, but as strangers. In other words, people who did not quite belong and who were not quite in possession of what had been promised to them, but who constantly renewed their sense of the reality of that promise in the chance encounters and disclosures of the journey they were already in the middle of. The 'theophanies' in Genesis, particularly the meeting of Abraham with the three strangers (Genesis 18), Jacob's dream at Bethel (Genesis 28:10–end) and his wrestling through the night with the man at Peniel (Genesis 32:22–end), combine many of the themes which are most relevant to the world of sector ministry. The sense of homelessness, the constant crossing and recrossing of boundaries, the need for hospitality, the importance of chance encounters, vision in the midst of darkness or in the heat of the day, the naming of something as holy but only with the benefit of hindsight, the piecing together of a spiritual journey through a series of clues and the growing sense of providence, these elements in the patriarchal stories all connect with the puzzling and obscure world sector ministers also inhabit.

Most sector ministers work with short-term contracts, meeting the needs of a transitory group of people. At the most a relationship will last a few years and many relationships can last an hour or less. To give each of these relationships their proper value requires a particular kind of spiritual awareness: the willingness to accept the stripping away of old certainties, for example. One is never sure when one has crossed the boundary between what is religious and what is secular. One is never sure what seeds of faith may be sown in the course of ordinary social contact, or when one particular activity is going to assume a special importance. One can go back to a familiar programme, certain of its success, and find that, with a different set of people, it does not work at all. A change in the timetable or the reorganization of departments may mean that the time for pastoral contact and worship disappears and one is forced to start again from scratch. The whole culture of the institution one is working in can change very quickly, as can that of the people passing through it, so that one is constantly searching for new means of access and learning new idioms. There is something about the position of the patriarchs, set adrift from their own gods and the customs of their own people and living on the edge of the customs and conflicts of other communities which suits us very well. In 'Little Gidding' T. S. Eliot beautifully conveys that dual sense of dispossession but potential for meaning inherent in the environment in which sector ministers operate.

The willingness to journey, and to give and receive hospitality are closely entwined. The more 'homeless', in that sense, one is oneself, the more willing to entertain the needs and hopes of others and to learn their language. The root for the words 'hostel' and 'hospital' is the same. These 'places of sojourn' were first set up in pilgrimage centres where travellers did not have the protection of their own family and customs. Abraham, the tent–dweller, a man of no fixed abode himself, entertains the strangers, allowing them to carry on their journey as he does on his. In the process he calls down on himself and his wife God's promise and blessing. In a mobile society where it is more and more in the nature of all relationships outside the immediate family to be transitory, such acts of hospitality are often the only ground on which the hope of community exists.

Hospitality is closely associated with the helping and healing rituals whereby we make another person feel at home. It is more a matter of gesture than it is of words, as Abraham's invitation to the strangers demonstrates (Genesis 18:3–8). Finding the right rituals for the right occasions in a context that is always changing is part of the sector minister's art. Hospitality in the highly pressurized environment of secular institutions carries with it the potential for worship. It creates the space for it. Our gestures become sacraments of an encounter not only with each other, but with God. So that, in Orthodox tradition, Abraham's act of hospitality is taken up and reversed to become a symbol of the hospitable nature of God. The three angels sitting beneath the oak at Mamre become an icon for the Trinity. In the generosity of that divine nature, consubstantial, coinherent and eternal, the icon implies, all things live and move and have their being. Any genuine act of hospitality creates the possibility of contact with the true nature of God. Any act of generosity and self-limitation puts us in contact with the divine nature which is at one and the same time self–emptying and self-fulfilling. Any moment of any day we may come into contact with that divine Reality through the quality of our human encounters, transitory though many of them are. Without that expectation it is hard to see how sector ministers can sustain a sense of calling in a ministry which constantly demands that they let go and move on and allow others to do the same.

> We shall not cease from exploration
> And the end of all our exploring
> Will be to arrive where we started
> And know the place for the first time.[3]

Notes

1 David Martin, *Times Literary Supplement* (29 August 1997), p. 7.
2 Ibid.
3 T. S. Eliot, 'Little Gidding', in *Collected Poems 1909–1962* (London: Faber & Faber, 1963), p. 222. Reproduced by kind permission of the publishers.

3

Sector ministry in a sociological perspective

Sophie Gilliat-Ray

Introduction

> Chaplaincy work as a sector ministry in the Church of England can very often become isolated from what goes on in parishes. Very often the Church authorities see the parish as the 'real' work of the Church.

This quotation is from a hospital chaplain in response to a questionnaire survey for 'The Church of England and Other Faiths Project,'[1] and his comment is by no means an isolated expression of isolation. Clergy who serve in sector ministries often feel that their work is unseen by the wider church, and they sense that their contribution to church debate and discussion about contemporary ministry is not heard. Working in the public institutions of this country such as prisons, hospitals and universities, those in sector ministries are largely removed and set apart from what is widely regarded as the 'real' work of the church, based in parishes. In some respects, their sense of isolation is not surprising given that only 7.7 per cent of ordained Anglican clergy currently serve in sector ministries full-time.[2]

Where parish clergy interface with relatively stable local communities and congregations, those in sector ministries interact with individuals and communities that are (a) often, like themselves, also 'set apart' in some way (e.g. in prison), and (b) are often in transition or only temporarily available for ministry (e.g. in hospital). Frequently, those who benefit from the work of sector ministers are people who, for whatever reason, are 'unchurched' or those whose circumstances have placed them outside the normal remit of parish ministry. These distinctive sociological characteristics of sector ministry place unique challenges and opportunities before those called to serve the church in these settings.

The quotation that opened this chapter indicated the sense of isolation from the rest of the church that those in sector ministries often feel. While it is true that many chaplains share this sense of being separate[3] from the church, at the same time plenty of others also regard themselves as being at the cutting edge of ministry and especially alert to the pastoral and ministerial questions of our time. Those in sector ministries argue that the challenging religious issues and trends in wider society are most sharply reflected in the contexts of sector ministry.[4] Within the very particular setting of a prison, hospital, forces or university chaplaincy, the social and religious patterns of society can be seen in microcosm, perhaps more clearly than within the parameters of a parish boundary. Similarly, the changing pressures and constraints that face those in sector ministries also serve as indicators of new expectations and developments in society. For example, the Patient's Charter injected a new consumer-driven approach into health-care provision, and chaplaincy services in hospitals have had to respond to new demands and expectations as a consequence. Like the institution of the church itself, the prison chaplain no longer carries the authority she once did, either for inmates, or within the hierarchy of the prison establishment, yet prison chaplains continue to have an integral and important pastoral role in penal institutions. Changing roles in sector ministry, in response to changes and developments in wider society and the church, also form an important part of the sociological discussion.

A church for the nation

Over the centuries the Church of England has had an integral relationship with other institutions in society. To some extent its identity is interwoven with that of the monarchy, the government and other public domains such as hospitals, schools, prisons and universities. Sector ministry has always been a dimension of this strong ongoing link between the church and public institutions, partly being a reflection of the implicit connection of Christian ministry with learning and teaching, pastoral care and healing. Historically, the established church has played an important role in social life and, contemporarily, the voice and influence of the church can be heard in public debate. The Church of England continues to be widely regarded as the national church, and the most representative religious body for people in England. 'In a country with significant regional identification, it could be argued that the Church of England is one of the few over-arching symbols of English, as opposed to British, identity.'[5] Everyone has an automatic right of access to its services, pastorally, liturgically and sacramentally. As the Archbishop of Canterbury expressed it: 'We are a national Church. This gives us immense privileges as well as responsibilities. The strength of being such a Church is that there is a recognisable parochial network throughout the land.

People have a right to call on us and seek the sacramental ministries of our Church.'[6]

Normally this access is made available through the parish system, and everybody, regardless of faith or denomination, falls within the geographical structure of parish boundaries. This is without doubt a very inclusive vision, and most parish churches continue to represent this taken-for-granted face of familiar, accessible, English religiosity. Similarly, though some types of sector ministry have a longer history than others, the focus of this ministry has always been across the whole institution. The 'parish' of the prison or hospital chaplain has been, and will no doubt continue to be, the whole prison or hospital community, including the staff.

Religious trends in society and sector ministry

Despite the fact that the church has a geographical and historical presence in every community, the number of people who now formally identify with it and regularly participate in its activities shows a steady and continuing decline. Though there are areas of growth, these are not yet strong enough to reverse the general trend away from regular churchgoing and active church belonging. Table 3.1 shows the precise areas of decline and growth in church attendance, but of course these statistics cannot measure the extent of continued *unconscious* identification with the church as a part of national, cultural heritage.

Table 3.1   *Church attendance in England by churchmanship, 1985–2000*[7]

England	1985	1990	1995	2000
Anglo-Catholic	137,000	127,800	123,000	123,200
Broad	342,000	321,200	299,600	289,600
'Catholic'[8]	1,521,400	1,464,200	1,217,300	1,091,000
Evangelical: Broad	317,600	314,900	298,500	292,500
Evangelical: Charismatic	370,000	397,300	412,600	432,100
Evangelical: Mainstream	249,100	254,200	256,400	262,800
Liberal	376,200	371,700	346,400	334,000
Low Church	214,700	205,500	190,600	183,200
All others	55,200	55,400	53,400	53,400
TOTAL	3,583,200	3,512,200	3,197,800	3,061,800

Note: The figures for the year 2000 are estimates.

Set against this gradual decline in regular church attendance, there has been a steady increase in the numbers of smaller Christian groups, sectarian movements, and other faith communities. Table 3.2 indicates the increase in other faith groups, as well as the decline in broadly Christian religious affiliation. Again, figures for the year 2000 are projected estimates.

Table 3.2 *UK religious community, 1975–2000 (in millions)*[9]

	1975	1980	1985	1990	1995	2000
Christian Trinitarian	40.2	39.8	39.1	38.6	38.1	37.8
Non-Trinitarian	0.7	0.8	1.0	1.1	1.3	1.4
Hindu	0.3	0.4	0.4	0.4	0.4	0.5
Jew	0.4	0.3	0.3	0.3	0.3	0.3
Muslim	0.4	0.6	0.9	1.0	1.2	1.4
Sikh	0.2	0.3	0.3	0.5	0.6	0.6
Other religions	0.1	0.2	0.3	0.3	0.3	0.3
TOTAL	42.3	42.4	42.3	42.2	42.2	42.2
Percentage of population (%)						
Christian Trinitarian	72	71	69	67	65	64
Non-Trinitarian	1	1	2	2	2	2
Non-Christian religions	3	3	3	4	5	6
Total all religions	76	75	74	73	72	72

From this very general picture of trends and patterns in national religious life, many of the same kind of observations can be said about sector ministry, historically and contemporarily. Regardless of religious belief or other affiliations, everyone has a right to the pastoral care of the sector minister, and this sense of 'availability' has characterized perceptions of sector ministry both within and outside institutions. Yet like the wider church, chaplains today rarely preach in chapels with a full congregation, and fewer patients in hospital or prisoners in jail now regard themselves as members of the church. The annual census of religious registrations among prisoners, between 1991 and 1997 (see Table 3.3), to some extent mirrors more widespread general trends in society. The figures betray an increase in religious diversity, but also an increasing number of prisoners who now register as 'no religion', 'agnostic' or 'atheist'. Whether this is actually due to changing religious attitudes, or whether chaplains are now more willing to record 'no interest in religion' (as opposed to a default categorization 'C of E') is impossible to assess. But in microcosm, Table 3.3 to some extent reflects wider social trends.

Tables 3.2 and 3.3 indicate that parish ministry and sector ministry (certainly within prisons) is now carried out in a context of increasing religious diversity. Nationally, however, there are strong regional variations in the extent of this diversity, and areas in the south-west of England contrast markedly with communities in the West Midlands conurbation, London or the large towns and cities in the north of England, in terms of the extent of diversity. It is estimated that 7 per cent of the population in the UK are members of faiths besides the Christian, but they are extremely unevenly

Table 3.3 *Annual census of religious registrations, prisoners in England and Wales, 1991–97*[1]

	1991	1992	1993	1994	1995	1996	1997	% of total in 1997	% change 1991–7
Main Christian[2]	32,991	33,532	30,334	31,858	30,300	34,452	36,498	62.92%	+11%
Other Christian[3]	644	682	668	719	651	486	527	0.9%	−18%
Main other faiths:									
Buddhist	183	192	177	168	182	230	226		+24%
Hindu	151	135	161	157	162	201	198		+31%
Jewish	194	203	209	198	178	203	288		+48%
Muslim	1,959	2,095	2,106	2,513	2,745	3,340	3,693		+89%
Sikh	307	313	323	363	353	381	394		+28%
Sub-total	2,794	2,938	2,976	3,399	3,620	4,355	4,799	8.27%	+72%
Other faiths	238	268	325	313	179	350	203	0.34%	−15%
Agnostic, Atheist									
None	6,866	7,609	7,415	10,405	11,420	13,556	15,840	27.3%	+130%
Non-permitted religions[4]	68	85	140	157	129	152	138	0.23%	+103%
Total	43,601	45,114	41,858	46,851	46,299	53,351	58,005	99.96%	+33%

1. Source: Taken from the *Annual Religious Census*, Prison Service Chaplaincy (PSC). The PSC's nomenclature and classification of religious groups is confusing and in some cases questionable

2. Church of England; Methodist; Church of Scotland; Protestant; Pentecostal; Baptist; Roman Catholic; Non-Conformist

3. Calvinist; Celestial Church of God; Church in Wales; Church of Ireland; Congregationalist; Coptic; Episcopalian; Ethiopian Orthodox; Orthodox (Greek/Russian); Presbyterian; Quaker; Salvation Army; Seventh-day Adventist; United Reformed Church; Welsh Independent; Other Christian; Christadelphian; Jehovah's Witnesses; Christian Science

4. Nation of Islam ('Black Muslim'); Rastafarian; Scientology

distributed across the country.[10] What is notable, however, is the extent to which this 7 per cent observe the traditions and norms of their faith. Despite the fact that there are no accurate figures for rates of mosque or temple attendance, I would suggest that members of groups who have recently immigrated are especially committed to their faith traditions.

There is no doubt that the increase in religious diversity in particular has presented pastoral and professional challenges to those in sector ministries. For example, other members of hospital, university or police staff may regard all matters to do with religion as the responsibility of the chaplain, but she may not have been trained to understand the specific needs of different religious communities. Complications and tensions can arise when it comes to such things as worship spaces or religious dietary requirements, and Christian chaplains may find themselves having to respond to new issues and meet new demands. But despite potential difficulties, there are many positive experiences derived from chaplaincy in multi-faith contexts. The comments of a group of hospital chaplains for the Church of England and Other Faiths Project reflect some of these. They noted that the presence of other faiths encouraged them to look to the individual needs of patients, particularly those needs that might be considered 'spiritual' as distinct from 'religious', and to have a more holistic approach to care. One chaplain put it like this: 'care of religious minorities is a paradigm for individualising care to all minorities and ultimately all patients and staff'. Another expanded on this point with the observation: 'We are beginning to recognise the *great variety of religious influences* on people. Many *younger people do not wish to be labelled in terms of religion*. The recognition of religious diversity might enable more appropriate and sensitive pastoral care to be given to individuals who are connected to a variety of religious communities' (emphasis added).

'Believing without belonging'

These comments about sector ministry and religious diversity highlighted in the quotation above further point towards other religious trends in wider society, and perhaps more accurately to the discrepancy between religious attitudes and feelings, as against measures of orthodox religious believing and belonging. In her book *Religion in Britain Since 1945*, Grace Davie notes that there is a marked difference between two types of variable in the measurement of religiosity. 'On the one hand, variables concerned with feelings, experience and the more numinous aspects of religious belief demonstrate considerable persistence in contemporary Britain; on the other, those which measure religious orthodoxy, ritual participation and institutional attachment display an undeniable degree of secularisation'.[11]

It is perhaps within the context of sector ministry that Davie's well-known phrase 'believing without belonging' is particularly well illustrated. There are many moving accounts from chaplains about their work with those who are 'unchurched', and those who do not regularly associate with a parish congregation. But there is also no lack of religious experience and feeling among those who are 'unchurched' whether they are the imprisoned, the sick or those who face the loneliness of long sea voyages. Such accounts are unlikely to show familiarity with formal religious vocabulary, and they are unlikely to be associated with past or current regular attendance at a place of worship. But they continue to provide evidence of ongoing 'common' religiosity, which perhaps may only become explicit at times of life crisis or transition.

What statistics about church attendance cannot indicate is the degree of spiritual awareness 'albeit unfocused and hesitant',[12] and the considerable ongoing emotional attachment to the church. People continue to turn to it at times of crisis, both locally and nationally, and many people when asked for their religion, for example on hospital forms, continue to identify themselves as C of E. This abiding, if latent, loyalty to the church amongst much of the population does not translate into regular attendance. In some ways this has led to a tension among clergy, between those who argue for an exclusive focus to Anglican ministry, and those who maintain the need for a church that is available to all.

> There is a collective feel that the present Church of England is under pressure, both financially and socially. Many of the clergy polled think that this is no bad thing and that the Church will be forced to concentrate on its role as a Christian missionary organisation in a pagan society. It will need to regroup, retrench, and discard its role of being a point of spiritual contact for the 'unchurched'. Others think that this is the very *worst* thing to do and that, using as many alternative forms of ministry as possible, the Church should maintain its role as the Church of all the nation for as long as possible.[13]

Non-parochial ministry is to some extent freed from these internal church tensions, since many of those in sector ministry are employees of the institutions that they serve, rather than of the church. But, paradoxically, while some parochial clergy are responding to the periodic (and, one senses, inconvenient) demands of the 'unchurched' by calling for a more congregational and exclusive focus to their ministry, the remit of prison chaplaincy (and apparently other forms of sector ministry) appears to be becoming more, not less, inclusive. Prison chaplains, for example, are generally regarded by others within the establishment as having overall responsibility for religious matters within the institution, including facilitating worship and pastoral care for prisoners and staff of *all* faiths, not just Anglicans or even Christians. Many prison chaplains defend this position as 'brokers' for other traditions on the grounds that Anglicanism necessarily has an inclusive tradition of ministry that is not denominationally or congregationally focused. It appears that the seeds of a dichotomy are emerging: between those in sector ministry whose work is necessarily becoming more inclusive, and a significant proportion of those in parish ministry who are calling for a more exclusive focus for parochial ministry. Nevertheless, the divergence in approach and attitude between the two groups is likely to be a different response to the same kind of pressures, challenges and changing religious trends taking place in wider society.

Another feature of contemporary religious expression can be seen in the way that people draw upon a wide variety of sources and resources to find inspiration and nourishment.

> Spiritual interests and concerns have become fragmented into separate spheres, each of which draws upon more profound and reflective aspects of the enthusiast's personality. The particular area of individual experience might relate to the natural world . . . the realm of music or the visual and creative arts . . . One cannot be other than impressed by the depth of individual commitment expressed, which clearly draws on feelings and opinions profoundly experienced, if often left formally unarticulated. Some of these commitments may come from faiths, Christian or otherwise, while much more comes from spiritual understandings that owe little or nothing to explicitly Christian doctrines. All too often churchmen make the extremely ill-informed and patronising assumption that those who express no faith live their lives in apathetic or superficial agnosticism. This could not be further from the truth.'[14]

A clear source of evidence for the truths of this quotation was the massive public response to the death of Diana, Princess of Wales. In many of the public and private expressions of grief, there was an emphasis upon the personal, the experiential and the subjective, drawing upon a huge range of different 'spiritual' as well as 'religious' sources. Given the general decline in church attendance and, presumably as a natural concomitant, a decline in familiarity with traditional religious vocabulary and ritual, it was not surprising that a good deal of public and private mourning was personalized, individual, spontaneous and unconnected to formal religious traditions. Never on such a large scale was the distinction and also the intermingling of 'folk' religion and 'official' religion perhaps seen so clearly in recent British history. Many of the boundaries and categories used by sociologists and historians to describe religion were broken down – 'official and popular, traditional and modern, religious and irreligious, secular and sacred, rough and respectable, imposed and indigenous.'[15] Cutting across divisions between and within faiths, gender, age and generation, the public mourning for Diana and the 'pilgrimage' to participate in her funeral typified something of the eclectic but deeply embedded spirituality of contemporary Britain.

Sector ministry and social changes

Over the past century, the well-established sector ministries have had to respond to changes in society, and to developments within the institutions that they serve. It would be naïve to assume that the decline in church attendance, the increase in religious diversity or the lessening authority of the church in public life would leave those in sector ministry untouched. The examples below, from prison and hospital contexts, indicate some of the changes that have taken place in the roles of sector ministers, as a consequence.

Historically, the Church of England played a dominant role in prison regimes, and often the chaplain was part of the authority structure of the institution.

> The great Victorian prisons were designed to have religion at their core. At the centre of most of them stands a Chapel, sometimes the size of a Cathedral, where all prisoners had perforce to come for Sunday worship . . . [T]he chapels remain, an enduring reminder of the original purpose of our prisons. They were designed, on a philosophical basis of Christianity and Utilitarianism, as factories of virtue . . . [O]fficers carried staves in one hand and bibles in the other. The chaplain was there to point the finger of accusation, to call to repentance, to work on the vulnerable as a technician of guilt.[16]

Chaplains no longer wield such power today and nor does Christianity occupy such a central stage in prison life. Church of England chaplains now have to share their dwindling authority with other Christian denominations, and increasingly with 'visiting ministers' of other faith communities. These developments are a direct reflection of the religious changes that have taken place in British society, and with them have come new challenges and opportunities. In a study of prison chaplains,[17] it was clear that, to some extent, chaplains are far from autonomous or omnipotent but are actually struggling to retain professional power in a system which has, over time, begun to marginalize them. Only by becoming more inclusive, and adapting to the changing religious make-up of the prison population, have prison chaplains been able to retain their recognized and long-standing role as chaplains to the whole institution. Unlike some of their parochial colleagues, in the context of publicly funded chaplaincy, a ministry focused exclusively on Anglicans, or even Christians, is no longer an option.

The growing inclusivity of sector ministry can also be seen in the hospital context. Hospital chaplaincy has had to respond to a growth in religious diversity, but also to a decline in regular chapel attendance by staff, patients, and families. In view of this, and given the advances in medical science and the ascendancy of scientific world-views in advanced industrial societies, one might expect a corresponding move away from religious values and reference points in contemporary health-care services. But this is not the case. There has been an increase in the number of whole-time hospital chaplains, from 183 in 1984 to 266 in 1990,[18] and the first of the nine National Charter Standards stated in the Patient's Charter, launched in 1991, specifies 'Respect for privacy, dignity and religious and cultural beliefs'. Not only does this place responsibility for spiritual care upon all health care staff, but it also suggests a more inclusive framework for chaplaincy. The press release which accompanied the Department of Health's guidelines issued in January 1992 on 'Meeting the spiritual needs of patients and staff: good practice guidance' (HSG (92) 2) emphasized the fact that the 'New Guidelines make explicit for the first time the need to provide for the needs of patients of all religions'.

In a sample of 107 hospital chaplains,[19] a large majority viewed the implementation of the Patient's Charter as a development in some way of a better response to Christian *and* other faith patients, and an affirmation of spirituality in the hospital setting. They stressed terms such as 'accessibility', 'enabling' and a recognition of the inherent spirituality of all patients. They emphasized a need for an 'awareness of all patients' spiritual and religious needs' and being *available to all patients regardless of their faith, or lack of faith*. The accent was very much upon the 'spiritual' rather than the narrowly 'religious'.

Another way in which chaplains have had to respond to the changing climate wrought by NHS reorganization can be seen in the way that they now have to be able to prove the cost-efficiency of their departments. They have to be able to give an account for their services. Certainly this was challenging for many of them, since the provision of spiritual and pastoral care clearly cannot be easily measured or quantified. Nevertheless, meeting this challenge had resulted in positive outcomes as far as some were concerned. Many chaplains felt that the new consumer-driven climate of health-care provision in England, had ultimately led to a higher profile for chaplaincy services. With this increasing profile, and the necessity for accountability, came a responsibility to bring a more 'professional' approach to spiritual care. Some chaplains in the same sample resented the amount of time taken up with paperwork and the formulation of 'business plans', while others apparently welcomed the fact that, across the institution, chaplaincy was being taken more seriously. They considered the investment of their time in promoting a business-like image and profile for the chaplaincy as worthwhile, and they welcomed the recognition – on a par with other departments – as evidence that chaplaincy was regarded as a 'front-line' service.

Reviewing these findings in the light of an earlier quotation (see note 13), there appears to be a growing difference between the self-image of those in sector ministry, certainly in hospitals, and the self-perceptions of some parochial clergy who feel wearied by the continued calls upon them from the 'unchurched'. This is particularly evident when it comes to their sense of influence and status within their working environments. In his survey of 500 parochial clergy,[20] Ted Harrison found that 'many clergy appear to see themselves at the moment as members of a minority faith at odds with the world'. This contrasts markedly with the comments of many hospital chaplains about their work, and their more confident professional image within the hospital community: 'As a full-time chaplain I was "made" a manager. This has increased my status in hospital. I have greater communication with the managerial staff in general and particularly with the Chief Executive and senior managers. I can exert greater influence on spiritual issues.' Whether the need to accommodate to these changes is regarded as (a) a necessary and professional response to secular demands that need not affect the quality or essence of spiritual care, or (b) as a 'secularizing' of chaplaincy in the face of these demands, will no doubt become a matter of debate amongst those in sector ministry in the future.

The future of sector ministry

Given the expressions of isolation coming from those in sector ministry, it is perhaps surprising to find that among Anglican ordinands there is considerable interest in this type of ministry. In a 1996–97 study of final-year ordinands in the Church of England,[21] respondents were asked to identify areas of ministry to which they felt called for the future (see Table 3.4). There was an interesting distribution between the different types of sector ministry from those who expressed an interest in chaplaincy-type work later in their careers.

Based on 200 responses, 39 ordinands (19.5 per cent), expressed a specific interest in future sector ministry. Compared to the nearly 8 per cent currently employed in this area, future recruitment prospects look promising, particularly in the field of education. Some respondents indicated why they felt especially drawn to sector ministry, and again there was considerable diversity. Four respondents had identified sector ministry as an area to which they *felt a calling*, and this was usually the result of *having done a placement* in a chaplaincy setting as part of their ordination training. Others expressed this

Table 3.4 *Interest in future sector ministry*

Prison chaplaincy	4
Hospital chaplaincy	1
Educational chaplaincy (schools and universities)	8
Rural chaplaincy	1
Hospice chaplaincy	2
Ministry in secular employment	9
Industrial chaplaincy	1
General sector ministry (unspecified)	13
TOTAL	39

sense of calling in different ways, by simply stating that they *felt suited* to this type of ministry, and that it was consonant with their experiences. A number of respondents were anticipating non-stipendiary ministry, but they saw this as an opportunity to share the gospel with colleagues as 'ministers in secular employment'. They felt that it was important to take pastoral care to a wider community, while another respondent felt he had 'a *responsibility to minister to all people*'. One ordinand expressed it directly as wanting 'to have one foot in the Church and the other in the world'. The appeal of other types of sector ministry included an *appreciation of its specialized nature*, the *one-to-one focus* and close contact with individuals, the more *structured working life* in sector ministry and '*more contact with the real world*'. Clearly, the increasing professionalism and inclusiveness demanded from those in sector ministry finds a resonance in the aspirations of some ordinands.

Though somewhat dated now, a study of Anglican clergy by Towler and Coxon[22] in 1979 sought to determine whether it was possible to predict which clergy might reach senior positions in the church, and at what point in their careers their choices become significant. They discovered that clergy who chose non-parochial ministry immediately after their curacy were in a strong position for gaining senior posts later in their careers. So it is from among ordinands who intend to move into sector ministry rather than to a benefice at the end of their curacy, that we are likely to find the next generation of senior clergy.

Notes

The author wishes to thank Preb. Paul Avis, Dr Grace Davie and Professor Jim Beckford for their helpful comments on an earlier version of this chapter.

1 Carried out in the Department of Sociology at the University of Warwick between 1994 and 1996 by Professor James Beckford and Dr Sophie Gilliat. The project investigated publicly funded chaplaincy (in prisons and hospitals) and civic religion. It was generously funded by the Leverhulme Trust and the Church of England.

2   Source: Advisory Board of Ministry, GS Misc 476, *Numbers in Ministry* (August 1996).

3   In a sample of 88 hospital chaplains as part of the Church of England and Other Faiths project (see note 1), 43 per cent felt that there was little or no evidence to suggest that their work was contributing to church debates.

4   Rather than chaplaincy work contributing to church debates, the views of some hospital chaplains were captured by the comment of one in particular: 'outside issues come into the hospital'.

5   Catherine Shelley, 'Why we need to free the Church from England', *Guardian* (21 February 1998).

6   George Carey, *Sharing a Vision* (London: Darton, Longman and Todd, 1993), p. 182.

7   *UK Christian Handbook – Religious Trends 1998/9*, no. 1, edited by Peter Brierley for 'Christian Research', p. 2.17. The table is based on the English Church Census for the 1985 and 1990 figures, adjusted for the actual attendance changes recorded, with 1995 and 2000 estimated from the proportions in each churchmanship category of each denomination in the census for 1989, given in Table 60 in *'Christian' England* (London: MARC Europe, 1991).

8   'Catholic' is in inverted commas to save confusion with Roman Catholics, who are only one component of this group, albeit a major component.

9   *Religious Trends*, op. cit., p. 2.3.

10   Ibid., p. 2.17.

11   Grace Davie, *Religion in Britain Since 1945: Believing Without Belonging* (Oxford: Blackwell, 1994), p. 4.

12   Ted Harrison, *Members Only? Is the Church Becoming Too Exclusive?* (London: Triangle/ SPCK, 1994), p. 2.

13   Ibid., p. 118.

14   Allen Warren, 'What future the Church of England?' in Allen Warren (ed.), *A Church for the Nation* (Leominster: Gracewing, 1992), p. 28.

15   David Hempton, 'Popular religion – 1800–1986' in T. Thomas, *The British: Their Religious Beliefs and Practices, 1800–1986* (London: Routledge, 1988), p. 202.

16   H. Potter, 'Speaking from the heart', *New Life*, 8 (1991), p. 67.

17   See note 1.

18   The Hospital Chaplaincies Council *Annual Report* to General Synod for 1985 included the following quotation from an article published in the *Health and Social Services Journal* on 'Treating mind, body and soul': 'Which group of NHS staff has doubled its numbers in the past ten years, scarcely raising a comment from the public and the government? Which group of staff did most patients in a survey say they would have liked to consult while in hospital? Which staff work a sixteen hour day on a public holiday, regardless of whether the hospital is full or not? Answer: hospital chaplains.'

19   See note 1. For more details about the project, contact the author.

20   Ted Harrison, *Members Only?* pp. 51 and 127.

21   'Theological education for a multi-faith Britain' was an 18-month study of how ordinands are being trained to work in multi-faith contexts, and how they are thinking theologically about religious diversity, carried out by Dr Sophie Gilliat at the University of Warwick between 1996 and 1997; the project was generously funded by the Leverhulme Trust. While the focus was upon Anglican theological colleges and courses, students from other denominations (e.g. Methodist and United Reformed Church) training at ecumenical colleges and courses authorized for Anglican ordination training were included in the survey. Questionnaires were distributed to all final year students; most respondents will now be in their first year of a curacy.

22   R. Towler and A. Coxon, *The Fate of Anglican Clergy: A Sociological Study* (London: Macmilllan, 1979).

PART TWO

Sector ministries

4

Agriculture

Anthony Russell

The historical link between church and countryside

It is remarkable that agricultural chaplaincy was almost the last of the specialist ministries to develop in the life of the church, considering that the church has had an intimate relationship with farming from its very beginning. For many centuries farming was not a specialist economic activity but the means by which everyone gained a livelihood, either directly or indirectly. As late as the eighteenth century many of the industrial enterprises, such as the naval dockyards at Portsmouth, stopped work at harvest time, so closely were urban and rural life still related. The division of England into an urban and a rural nation did not take place until the middle stages of the Industrial Revolution with the development of such specialist manufacturing cities as Sheffield. When Disraeli wrote of 'two nations' he was referring to the rich and the poor, but by the mid-nineteenth century he could have been referring to urban and rural England, so quickly had they become separated in social and economic terms.

The particular history of the church has given it a more intimate relationship with farming than with any other occupational activity. From the earliest period, when bishops gave Saxon thegns the right to appoint parish priests (the origins of patronage) the thegns were obliged to grant land to the priests (the origins of glebe), who also enjoyed rights to a share in the farming produce of the village (the origins of tithe). Tithe and glebe were the traditional means of providing financial support for the parish clergy and it is a monument to the pastoral wisdom and sensitivity of Anglican clergy that these potentially troublesome arrangements have left no legacy of rural anticlericalism in England. Therefore it was inevitable that the material fortunes of the Anglican clergy followed the prosperity of farming.

The fact that people lived and worked in the same community meant that the Victorian clergy related both to their residential and occupational lives. In the main the clergy were principally concerned with social issues rather than with commenting on the nature of farming at this time. The mid-eighteenth century (often referred to as the 'Agricultural Revolution') was a time of pioneer work in livestock farming and crop rotation. There were further advances in breeding and particularly in the mechanization of arable farming in the mid-nineteenth century in which the introduction of the threshing machine was among the most important. However, despite these changes, much farming remained traditional (the last ox man in Britain, Ted Smith of the Cirencester Park estate, retired in 1963).

During the Second World War the importance of agriculture was recognized as being vital in the fight for national survival. In 1939, Britain produced 30 per cent of its own food, but by 1945 the figure had risen to 80 per cent. During this period the percentage of farm land under cultivation nearly doubled and again approached the levels of the 1860s and 1870s. Though pioneer farm machinery had existed for some time (the first effective tractor, the Ival, was marketed in 1902 and the first combine harvesters appeared in 1928), the war saw a dramatic advance in mechanized agriculture. The introduction of scientific methods and mechanization, and the abandonment of traditional practices, turned farming into a professional occupation within a relatively short period. The church, once so congruent with the ways of traditional agriculture, began to realize that modern agriculture was a world about which it knew very little. A number of dioceses recognized that it was necessary to have specialist clergy who could relate to the new, advanced mechanized agriculture; it was this that led to the appointment of agricultural chaplains.

The development of agricultural chaplaincy

The history of agricultural chaplains falls into three periods; in the first period agricultural chaplaincy was modelled closely on industrial mission; a paper from the St Albans diocese in the mid-1970s when a chaplaincy was being established indicates this clearly:

> The chaplaincy for agriculture and horticulture in Bedfordshire and Hertfordshire, an extension of industrial mission, is part of the total Mission and Ministry of the Church which focuses on the agricultural and horticultural industries, and which attempts to understand and co-operate with God's will for society in the critical areas of food production, care of the countryside and the pastoral care of those involved. The work of this chaplaincy will be undertaken by a network of people involved in

the industry and the churches who will meet regularly to support one another and develop the work under the leadership of the chaplain who will be a member of the Industrial Mission Team.

The first appointments were made in Worcester and Lincoln in the late 1960s, followed in the early 1970s by appointments in Carlisle, Hereford, Canterbury and Rochester. Agricultural chaplaincy saw farming as an industry which, though significantly different, bore increasing comparisons with other industries and therefore it was appropriate to apply the ideology and insights of industrial mission. Three of the early agricultural chaplains came directly from appointments in industrial chaplaincy.

Agricultural chaplains soon became involved in the major issues which faced the farming community; of these the intensification of livestock husbandry and more general concern for animal welfare were perhaps the most important. In the mid-1960s a number of books, including Ruth Harrison's *The Animal Machine*, had raised public awareness of the implications of intensification and this had resulted in the production of welfare codes for farm animals in 1968.

The Arthur Rank Centre was established in 1972, sponsored by the churches (acting ecumenically), the Royal Agricultural Society of England and the Rank Foundation. Under its first director, Canon Peter Buckler, the Centre soon became a significant bridge between the farming community and the churches at a national level. Canon Buckler was soon joined by another Anglican priest, a Methodist minister and a United Reformed Church minister. In a relatively short time the Arthur Rank Centre became a natural focus for the work of the agricultural chaplains, who met there regularly for mutual support and the exchange of information and ideas. An independent initiative started by a United Reformed Church minister, the Revd Philip Eastman, the Institute of Rural Life at Home and Overseas, also provided another focus for activity, including a major annual conference and a journal.

In this early period the agricultural chaplains still kept close to the industrial mission model; many of them were active members of the Industrial Mission Association. As with other industrial chaplains, agricultural chaplains sought connections with the work being done in Europe and were represented on the working group on agriculture and rural society of the European Ecumenical Commission for Church and Society. This group produced a major submission to the World Council of Churches' Conference on 'Justice, Peace and the Integrity of Creation'. At this time, the agricultural chaplains organized visits to Brussels and Strasbourg and meetings with European leaders and also to France and Bavaria. At the same time there was increasing contact with American and Canadian rural clergy and a number of visits were made by groups of agricultural chaplains at this period.

During this early period agricultural chaplains saw themselves exercising a pastoral and prophetic role to the farming community in the tradition of industrial mission. They related closely to the institutions and focal centres of the farming world in their counties, but often found themselves operating on two fronts. On one side, they tried to raise some of the moral and ethical issues which were increasingly concerning church people within the farming community; on the other, they sought to explain the life and work of the farming community to a church increasingly dominated by an urban ethos and agenda.

The second decade of agricultural chaplaincy saw a significant widening of the issues in which agricultural chaplains were involved. The 1970s had seen 'a quiet revolution' in the countryside as a result of the impact of population migration and the subsequent *embourgeoisiement* of rural villages. No longer was the village an isolated community comprised principally of those who worked on the farms and those whose families had lived in the village over many generations. Increasingly, the village was populated by 'new villagers' – the commuters, the retired and second-home owners. Between 1951 and 1961, the rural population increased by 0.6 million but between 1961 and 1971 the increase was 1.6 million. However, the impact on rural areas varied and there were still many rural areas which were losing population. Conferences on 'rural depopulation' were held as late as the 1970s in Norfolk. But in most rural areas, after the mid-1960s, there was a rapid growth when the number moving into villages was twice the number of those leaving.

The churches realized that the changes which were taking place in the countryside, and the new systematic approach that was being adopted to these changes by local authorities, required them to have somebody who could relate to these issues. At the same time the Church of England had been made aware by the Paul Report (1968) of the need to adapt its own structures and deployment in such a way that they would relate to the changes taking place in English society, particularly in urban areas. As a consequence of the Paul Report, the church sought to address the imbalance of clergy deployment between rural and urban areas and effectively to shift the balance in favour of urban areas. For the countryside it recommended new strategies, particularly the development of group and team ministry, which was already being pioneered in Lincolnshire and Norfolk.

The church was aware both of the disproportionate deployment of clergy between urban and rural areas and of a relatively steep decline in the number of stipendiary clergy (between 1961 and 1984 the total number of full-time Anglican clergy fell from approximately 15,000 to approximately 11,000). The declining number of clergy was having an effect on church life but the processes of change were slow and there were still clergy (often elderly) looking after very small parishes. One correspondent to Leslie Paul's question-naire had a parish of only 220 people; another wrote: 'The parish is not a full time job ... It is easy to find oneself gently rotting away.' It was these circumstances that the church sought to address in the 1970s, and following the County Structure Plans many of the dioceses developed Diocesan Pastoral Strategies for the rationalization and redeployment of the church's resources. The dioceses needed an officer to do the detailed work (in consultation with the County Planning Department) and to assist in the process of persuading parishes and deaneries to adopt the recommendations. In many dioceses the agricultural chaplain became increasingly involved in issues of pastoral reor-ganization and this matter occurs frequently in the minutes of the agricultural chaplains group during this period. Slowly almost all agricultural chaplains moved away from an exclusive concern with ministering to the farming community and became involved in wider issues which affected the countryside.

A further example of the way in which the concerns of agricultural chaplains diversified in the 1980s was their involvement in the establishment of training schemes for the unemployed, whose numbers had risen consider-ably, funded by the Manpower Services Commission.

For many years those ministering in the rural church had felt that the issues and concerns of the countryside had been ignored by the church at a national and diocesan level and that they were ministering in the church's 'second eleven'. If anything these feelings were heightened during the 1980s, when the attention of the church was focused on the landmark document *Faith in the City*. The subsequent determination of the church to address the problems of urban priority areas and to raise money to extend the church's ministry in these areas and to support community development work through the Church's Urban Fund all served to heighten the rural church's feelings of marginality.

The agricultural chaplains played a major role in persuading the church of the need for a parallel initiative in rural areas. Initially this met with little positive response from church leaders and the Standing Committee of the General Synod of the Church of England effectively decided not to support this initiative. However, there was increasing evidence that the rural areas of the church felt neglected and such an initiative would play a significant role in focusing the concerns of the rural church and analysing some of the wider issues which currently faced the countryside. The determination of Peter Nott, the Bishop of Norwich, and the agricultural chaplains was focused in a Green Paper debated by General Synod in 1987. In that year the Archbishop of Canterbury (Lord Runcie) accepted an invitation to preach at the Royal Show service and in his sermon acknowledged the extent to which the focus of the church's concern had been in urban areas and announced the setting up of a Rural Commission. Twenty-one people from a diverse variety of backgrounds and experience accepted the invitation of the Archbishops of Canterbury and York to be members of the Commission, and Ewan Harper and the Revd Jeremy Martineau were invited to act as the joint secretaries. The Commission sat for two years and combined hearing of evidence in London with a substantial programme of rural visits and the commissioning of research and papers. The eventual report *Faith in the Countryside* was published in 1990. It was widely acknowledged as an authoritative statement on the present situation in rural areas, and a lengthy list of recommended actions was enjoined upon the state and the churches. Without doubt this was an important document and almost all subsequent reports on rural areas have acknowledged its significance.

There were four immediate consequences; first, the report provided a focus for the discussion of rural issues and the church's place in the countryside. It was now widely acknowledged that the church was alongside those organizations seeking to assist and help in addressing the problems of rural areas. Second, it led to the appointment of a link officer in each diocese whose task was to promote local study of the report and to implement its recommendations. Third, the report demonstrated to other rural organizations the extent to which the church was determined to approach the issues and problems of the countryside. Previously the church had been thought to be dominated by a landowning, patrician approach to rural areas and a 'horse-drawn' approach to agriculture. Fourth, the Archbishop appointed the Revd Jeremy Martineau to be his rural officer. It is the ancient wisdom of parochial ministry that if something is to be done there must be a person to make it happen. The Archbishop's Rural Officer acted as an important national focus for the church's concern for rural areas and for the implementation of the recommendations of the report. Mr Martineau joined the staff at the Arthur Rank Centre and was instrumental in establishing the magazine *Country Way*, which has been an important focal point for a discussion of the issues which agricultural chaplains now addressed.

At this time the number of full-time chaplains declined and their posts frequently became part-time appointments. Almost every diocese now had somebody acting in the role of rural or agricultural chaplain but fewer of these appointments were full time and some of them were effectively a role added to a significant pastoral responsibility.

The early 1990s saw the beginning of a turnaround in the fortunes of the agriculture industry; although these were prosperous years, far-sighted observers of the agricultural scene could already see the problems that lay ahead. However, nobody could have forecast the extreme problems that resulted from the BSE epidemic. As a consequence of this change, the work of many agricultural and rural chaplains was refocused on the rural community and particularly on the pastoral and social consequences of the downturn in farm incomes and the widespread evidence of distress within the farming community. This may be regarded as the beginning of the third period in the development of agricultural chaplaincy.

Anxiety in the farming community increased with the election in May 1997 of a new British government which was seen to be less knowledgeable and concerned about rural areas in general, and the farming community in particular, together with changes in the financial arrangements of the European Common Agricultural Policy which have resulted in a drop in farm incomes. Increasingly attitudes towards the countryside and farming are shaped by the immensely powerful conservation and animal rights organizations (there are over 30,000 registered animal welfare charities) and the way in which the environment and farming are treated in schools and in the media. These feelings of marginalization were expressed in two major rallies in London in 1997/98 which brought together people wishing to protest on a range of rural issues.

At the same time a number of highly publicized food scares, culminating in the complications associated with BSE, first identified in the mid-1980s and linked to 'new variant' CJD in March 1996, further affected the farming community. Few occupations have seen such a dramatic change in public esteem: a generation ago farmers were regarded as national heroes, whose efforts saved the country from starvation; today they are vilified in the media as despoilers of the landscape, destroyers of habitat, slaughterers of wild life, prohibiters of access to those who wish to roam the fields and greedy developers anxious to sell what remains of rural England. As a consequence, farmers have come to regard themselves as a marginalized group in an increasingly hostile environment. The symptoms of stress within the farming community are manifested by the fact that it now has more suicides than any other occupational group. Today many agricultural chaplains work closely with the Rural Stress Information Network established at the Arthur Rank Centre, where its director is seconded from the National Farmers Union. This organization co-ordinates county-based initiatives which seek to help and befriend those faced with the stress of modern farming.

Conclusion

Thus it can be seen that agricultural chaplaincy, which has sought to offer a pastoral and a prophetic ministry to the agricultural and rural community, has passed through a number of stages. In the first period, the 1970s, it was principally concerned with demonstrating the church's involvement and care for a farming community which had been changed so dramatically as it transferred from traditional to modern agricultural practices. In the 1980s, the role of many agricultural chaplains began to widen and it was at this time that many appointments became known as Rural Officers. The church's own agenda and the progress of pastoral reorganization, together with the changes taking place in the rural community, had the consequence of redirecting the work of chaplains towards a broader agenda and a wider involvement in the issues of the rural community. In the 1990s, the *Faith in the Countryside* agenda came to dominate the concerns of rural and agricultural chaplains and, as the decade progressed, rural issues rose steadily up the political agenda. Those who live in the countryside have come to feel marginalized in an increasingly urban society which they feel does not understand their concerns and lifestyle.

The church's task is to proclaim and prefigure the kingdom of God by announcing the gospel to the world and by its existence as the body of Christ. In every decade agricultural chaplains have sought to do this as a specialist ministry within the churches and to be a bridge between the rural community in general, and the farming community in particular, and the life and work of the churches.

5

Airports

Michael Vincer

An unusual place?

'So you're an airport chaplain, but what do you do?' This is not an untypical
start to an introductory conversation. I am not sure whether the statement
should end with a question mark or exclamation mark; either way it causes me
some confusion. I have plenty to do, but to list a host of activities could give
the wrong impression and possibly present a disharmony of purpose and
function. What prompts the questioner to ask in this particular way? What
impression does it present of their perceptions of ministry and mission? I am
on occasions blessed with some helpful suggestions – do you walk around the
terminals looking for lost souls, or stand on the runway blessing aircraft? I
have done neither of those things and, to the best of my knowledge, neither
have any of my colleagues.

The essence of airport chaplaincy is much the same as ministry elsewhere
– to serve others in the name of Christ. This is in response to the loving and
compassionate God who calls all baptized people into service. The nature of
that response will be defined by activities appropriate to the place. I am there
to celebrate creative manifestation of skills and gifts used in the service of
others; to question and challenge strategies and practice that negate humanity.
I am there to serve, and address need. What intrigues most people about the
work is not the nature of ministry but the place where it is exercised. Perhaps
the question is rarely asked of chaplains in other areas of work. It will seldom
be asked of parish ministers – well-defined assumptions are made about their
work.

So what constitutes ministry and mission? I believe they comprise three
specific elements: pastoral, liturgical and prophetic; the first two are well
understood, the third is more contentious. The first is a natural response to

demonstrate love, care and compassion to neighbour and to God. The second is the public and corporate demonstration of thanksgiving, responsibility, confession, praise and intercession. The third is the response to those things identified as being contrary to God's love, God's will and God's justice: to see those marginalized, oppressed, undervalued and to address the causes with theological resourcefulness, love and courage.

This is the context of any ministry. It is the context of the ministry of airport chaplains, local in application and international in scope. Chaplains of all churches, and in some places of other faiths, are found at most of the world's major international airports, particularly in western Europe, North America and Australasia.

The origins of airport chaplaincy

During the mid-1940s chaplains serving with airborne forces, particularly at civil airfields, became aware of a potentially wider aspect to their ministry. Edwin Hogg, compiling a brief history of the International Association of Civil Aviation Chaplains (IACAC), acknowledged the phenomenal growth in aviation which had taken place. An employee of the US-based Eastern Airlines, he saw the need for an airport ministry to serve both employees and travellers. Airport terminal buildings should cater for the spiritual and practical needs of people, and provide places for prayer, meditation and counselling. He identified specific requirements that have become the principles by which most contemporary chapels and prayer rooms operate:

- a place set aside for individual prayer and meditation
- a place of stillness, a welcome oasis amid the constant activity
- a place which is always open, affirming the many faiths represented at international airports
- a chaplain available to serve the needs of those who work at or pass through airports.

The Roman Catholic Church was instrumental in establishing the first chaplains, under the guidance and care of the Vatican's Pontifical Council for the Pastoral Care of Migrants and Itinerant People. Development during the 1950s was relatively slow, and it was not until 1967, following the vision for a wider network of chaplains, that Father Xavier de Meeus of Brussels and Father Steux of Paris–Orly convened the inaugural meeting of the IACAC. Father Xavier's pioneering work, spanning thirty years, is acknowledged by the Association: it established the network of chaplains called to serve worker and traveller within the activity of international civil aviation.

The main objective of the Association is 'to enable the ecumenical group of chaplains in their priestly, pastoral, and prophetic ministry to, and with, people who work at and use civil airports'. Its purpose is 'to nurture ecumenical and spiritual relationships in the world'. From the early 1960s, as air travel increased and became more accessible to a greater number of people, airport chaplaincy became firmly established. By 1999 there were chaplaincies at 100 international airports, staffed by over 100 part-time or full-time chaplains, in many cases supported by significant numbers of volunteers. While the majority of these chaplains represent the main Christian denominations, there are an increasing number of airports which have chaplains of other faiths; a response to the essence of international travel which facilitates exchange between people of different cultures.

The need to foster an international network of chaplains is affirmed in the Association's principles:

- to provide and promote fellowship under God for those engaged in ministry in the unique environment of civil aviation
- to provide a continuing exchange of experience and insights to enhance the fulfilment of the task
- to develop understanding of how civil aviation functions, its effect upon people engaged in it and using it, and its influence in shaping the world
- to engage in mutual theological and sociological study, and reflection relevant to the task
- to affirm and communicate our experience of God's world which is given to us through the nature of civil aviation and our involvement in it
- to nurture ecumenical and spiritual relationships.

The airport culture

I believe it is the uniqueness of airports, their sense of purpose as well as their air of mystery, which prompts people to ask the 'What do you do?' question. Airports are without doubt different from many of the normal day-to-day experiences of most people. Apart from those whose business requires them to fly frequently, it is the experience of most others that flying equates with sun, sea and sand (or snow, piste and après-ski). Airports are points of departure for holiday, for relaxation and for recreation. They contain anticipation, anxiety, hope, concern, pressure; all affecting different people in different ways. For many it is an enjoyable and positive experience but for others it can be anything but, with anger, frustration and disappointment colouring memories best forgotten.

The perception of an airport will depend on one's experience. Passengers see the bright, clean and sparkling side of the industry, a somewhat 'sexy' atmosphere with people smartly dressed, activity very purposeful and focused, a general willingness to be friendly and helpful. However there is another side, a working environment of long hours, low pay, unpleasant working conditions, uncertain future, short-term contracts and constant pressure.

To perceive the nature of airport life it is necessary to strip away the glossy and ephemeral elements that can obscure reality. Airports can be places of: meeting/separation, life/death, hope/fear, pleasure/pain, justice/injustice, escape/captivity, health/sickness, joy/sorrow, peace/anger, liberation/delay, security/threat, crowds/solitude, movement/stillness, trust/suspicion, love/hate, plenty/poverty, certainty/doubt, tranquillity/upheaval, harmony/frustration, information/ignorance, affirmation/denial, freedom/detention, confidence/anxiety, laughter/tears, time/eternity.

These are part of the experiences and memories of air travel. Seasoned flyers will have experienced many of the above. For holidaymakers there is the difference between a memorable holiday and an experience which distorts relationships, leaves unhealed wounds about people and places, with the enduring vow to 'never again . . .'.

As a working environment there are significant differences in patterns of work that place stress on people, their families and their holistic engagement with life generally. The dimension in which decisions, competition and service standards are perceived is international, and the pressure to be 'The World's Best' is enticing (the 'World's Best Airport' accolade is given following an annual international survey conducted by IATA among a cross-section of all air travellers). Whilst such an accolade may be a matter of pride, it is also a fillip to competition, both nationally and internationally, for the provision and development of routes and services. This in turn places pressure on service companies competing for contracts, with knock-on effects for workers. Competition can be severe and, when subject to short-term contractual agreements, may place added pressure on wages and conditions of service. Seasonal working is a fact of life for many, particularly at airports with a high proportion of holiday and charter traffic. To work in this environment makes long-term family and financial planning a delicate balancing act. Life beyond the airport is significantly influenced by such stressful circumstances. Passengers will rarely perceive the tensions and pressure experienced by staff in the exercise of their duties. Staff have to bear verbal, and occasionally physical, abuse from angry, frustrated, drunk or simply anxious travellers.

It is sometimes too easy for the affirmation of human dignity, a fundamental element of God's relationship with us, to be overlooked. Even if this is unintentional on the part of the worker or traveller, there is a constant need to work for positive relationships and the maintaining of values rooted in the love God has shown to us. The pressure to maximize profit can lead to a seemingly selective approach when it comes to the care, nurture, development and value of staff. Responding to this culture creatively and with loving purpose is a significant aspect of an airport ministry. The circumstances require a response that is both proactive and reactive: the former by developing programmes of pastoral care and liturgical response, the latter through a constant awareness of what is going on, knowing others and being known by them. Chaplaincies have an advantage in this respect, as people make basic and positive assumptions about trust, integrity and the approachability of chaplains. While one cannot interfere with company decisions, there is room for a creative involvement on specific matters through developed trust.

It is important therefore that chaplaincies take every opportunity to become structurally integrated within the whole airport operation. Participation in organizational networks, showing commitment to people on their terms rather than one's own, without compromising creed or standards, are ways of working which others value. It gives marvellous opportunities to present a chaplaincy which proclaims the gospel of love through committed service and involvement. It is no longer a surprise to me (although it remains a pleasure inspiring humility) how ready many companies are to have a purposeful chaplaincy involvement with their operation.

The style and emphasis of the ministry

The nature of ministry has already been referred to as being primarily pastoral, prophetic and liturgical. It is essential, however, to understand that the ministerial origins and experiences of individual chaplains in their call to this work have significant influences on their particular styles of ministry. It cannot be assumed that a chaplaincy at one airport is identical to that at another.

Some chaplaincies, particularly in the UK, have their origins in industrial mission where the emphasis is on working with and alongside staff. This can naturally encourage a prophetic emphasis which influences the nature of pastoral and liturgical involvement. Chaplains from a predominantly parochial or sacramental background, however, may concentrate on pastoral and liturgical work. As in any ministry which aims to be comprehensive, all are necessary, and the more 'successful' teams are those whose work is strategically developed with this broad vision of service to the permanent and itinerant community. A particular influence on the style of ministry is the distinction between staff and passengers. The majority of major international airports usually have more than 10,000 staff, working for a large number of individual companies and covering a wide range of activities. Despite this diversity and independence there is a bond that links most people in a 'common cause': to ensure the timely departure and arrival of aircraft and the swift, purposeful and courteous movement of people. While one should not be too romantic about inter-company co-operation, it does exist, and is an activity where partnership in the service of others is rightly acknowledged. Here is cause for celebration in the workplace – mutual and purposeful commitment, in practical conjunction with the application of skill and ability in the service of others.

An understanding of the fundamental difference between staff and passengers is essential because an effective ministry must be adopted to serve both distinct 'groups'. Staff are permanently based at the airport, while passengers are there usually for a relatively short time. Exceptions must also be acknowledged, for they present a third area for consideration: flying staff from other airports, and passengers whose time at an airport is significantly extended by delay, misfortune or personal tragedy. This may seem to be stating the obvious; however, in common with any place where ministry is carefully planned, it is necessary to distinguish between the different requirements of each group and the best ways of fulfilling an appropriate ministry in each case. What might be appropriate for staff, with whom a long-term relationship of service can be developed in association with their respective companies, is not possible with passengers whose needs, requests and demands usually require immediate attention. These variations give rise to a haphazardness in ministry, which while all right on occasions, can present difficulties in the long term because there is little strategy to such activity. This variety of demand and response requires the maintaining of positive relationships with a chaplain's parent denomination, as well as the development of local ecumenical links. Such contacts must have a creative dynamic that avoids the sense of isolation so easily perceived. It requires personal effort on the part of the chaplain, proper management of the chaplaincy service and creative pastoral awareness by the relevant denomination, to ensure that this ministry is seen as part of the church's corporate response to the whole of society in which it is rooted.

The pastoral, prophetic and liturgical activity of ministry

Pastoral care has three distinct areas of activity: passengers and members of the public, emergency planning, and staff. Life for those working at or passing through an airport is as varied as life anywhere. Spiritual needs, as well as practical requirements, demand that chaplains respond in full knowledge of the services available in a complex and confusing environment. One important thing chaplains can provide is time: time to give to people to restore their equilibrium, to solve difficulty, to arrange onward care, to celebrate, to comfort, to counsel and simply to be with people where they are in their lives at that moment. The importance of this element of ministry cannot be overstated. The potential to spend time with individuals is in short supply in a schedule-driven, demanding environment.

Here are opportunities for the love we receive from God to be extended to others. Here is the opportunity to care for the hungry, the unloved, the bereft, the prisoner, the grieving, the confused, the lost. It is a crucial role, an enormous opportunity and exceptional privilege, for the church to respond to: to perceive need, to welcome, to give hope and to pray. This identification is an essential aspect of pastoral chaplaincy work. It can restore a sense of purpose to the lost and confused, direct events for the benefit of the traveller and make contact with friends and family. There is continuing demand to meet the bereaved, visit refugees or asylum seekers held in detention and be a visible presence throughout the airport.

Most chaplaincies are involved in emergency planning. This involves specialist areas of counselling and knowledge of the readily accessible networks of the church and various outside agencies. It requires chaplains to work in partnership with external emergency and support agencies, as well as with teams of local clergy alerted for emergency call-out. The origins of the chaplaincy, representing an organization firmly rooted in the community beyond the airport, can provide significant assistance, enabling creative contact to be made through well-established networks. Chaplains become a link between the airport and external agencies, able to help with their knowledge of airport practices and procedures, and enabling comprehensive assistance and comfort to those who require it. This care can extend long after an incident is over and will frequently involve long-term contact with staff, passengers or members of the public.

The third area of pastoral care is more proactive. Among staff, those with whom one has the greatest ongoing contact, programmes can be devised to serve their needs in a complex community. It is often the case here that those who have lost touch with the local church seek 'the God person' at the airport. This helps restore relationships between individuals and God, by encouraging local spiritual and practical support through liaison with the parish clergy. Working in partnership with those beyond the airport is vital in the provision of a comprehensive ministry. Liaison with local churches helps foster good relationships between the airport and the community, a positive contribution to communication with people living nearby who often feel overwhelmed by an airport's presence.

Workplace visiting is an essential aspect of pastoral work with staff and over time the regular and visible presence of a chaplain builds relationships of trust on which confidences are shared and help sought. As chaplains get to know people in their work, that awareness is raised about issues where people are taken for granted, undervalued or treated unfairly. This feeds the prophetic role of chaplaincy, demanding thoughtful and prayerful consideration as to appropriate action and identification of allies in the process. To spend time with people, to shadow them in their work, gives valuable insights into individual competence and commitment, and a greater bond between chaplain and workplace.

There is also the opportunity to reflect these experiences in worship. In a place where it can be difficult to tell which day of the week it is, the rhythm of regular worship plays an important part in restoring a sense of calm, tranquillity and purpose. Someone described an airport as being a place of organized chaos and eternal busy-ness. In this context, focusing on the transcendent and numinous, however briefly, re-establishes personal perceptions and awareness. Chaplaincies will approach this in a variety of ways. Those at major airports, especially in Christian countries, will often have the benefit of chapels or prayer rooms. The latter are used in some places to reflect their availability to people of all faiths. It acknowledges the nature of the community served by airports, as well as that essential aspect of international travel; the facilitation of exchange between peoples. This provision of space depends largely on the vision of the airport management company because the room is normally provided rent free. The 'facility' contributes to peoples' experience of an airport and the rooms are highly valued as oases of calm and quiet.

Regular celebrations of the Eucharist are held at many airports, together with daily prayerful routines, embracing through intercession the variety of abilities which enable air travel. Pilgrim groups will frequently use the chapels and prayer rooms; specific and emotive moments on a spiritual, as much as a physical, journey. The presence of chaplains integrated with the airport offers opportunity to conduct special services. Members of staff often wish to acknowledge the life of a colleague whose funeral they were unable to attend because of their duties. This presents an appropriate opportunity for reflection at a memorial service, affirming not only a former colleague, but their own work too. Periodically there may be celebrations of thanksgiving and reflection of the history and hopes of the airport. As airports develop – historic parts demolished and new buildings dedicated – creative affirmation of skill and ingenuity, and responsibility to the wider community, can be expressed.

Conclusion

There is a rule of thumb in civil aviation that for every million passengers there are approximately a thousand employees. Chaplaincies operating in this commercially driven environment – itself a product of human aspiration and ingenuity – have to develop ministries that are not only culturally appropriate but which provide relevant responses to the people they seek to serve. This is no different from any strategy for ministry and mission, but the question 'What do you do?' suggests that this approach is not readily understood. One chaplaincy, conducting a review of its services in conjunction with its airport authority, reached the conclusion that one full-time chaplain, or other appropriately qualified professional, is required for every five to six thousand staff.

Mindful of the 'one thousand to one million' ratio, they will also serve the five to six million passengers, as well as a similar number meeting, greeting and bidding goodbye. This suggests that most chaplaincies are underresourced and consequently may have difficulty in establishing strategies that offer a comprehensive airport-wide ministry. In many ways this is no different from ministry anywhere: choices have to be made, some things done and some left undone. It is vital however that this is acknowledged. Whether the chaplaincy is a lone person or a team, because of the creative activity that ministry should be, there is the danger that chaplains can become overwhelmed by a feeling of not fulfilling the task. Proper management and support of the individual or team, whatever the circumstances, are essential.

Chaplaincies at airports are only one aspect of the church's holistic ministry embracing the community. The pressure on the church to resource such ministry has to be seen in the context of the church's ability to serve the whole of the community, not only at airports. The challenge is to explore new ways of resourcing chaplaincy which draw others from the community served into its funding and management. The church's current financial and ministerial situation strongly indicates the benefit of a partnership with the airport served in the provision of a comprehensive and relevant chaplaincy.

6

Armed forces

Stephen Ware

The hardest place

'For war is the hardest place: if comprehensive and consistent moral judgements are possible there, they are possible everywhere.'[1] A major problem faced by military chaplains is that many involved in Christian ministry believe that war is fundamentally outside the scope and control of Christian morality. Consequently, military chaplains can be considered as having betrayed the gospel and have deluded themselves into believing that it is possible to provide Christian ministry to a situation which is as far removed from Christian principles as it is possible to be. This is the tension which many military chaplains are constantly working to resolve.

Background and history

The origins of military chaplaincy do not assist chaplains in resolving the tension. The earliest clerics involved in war, at least in Great Britain, were not involved in their priestly capacity but as feudal lords and military leaders. In the early part of the fourteenth century, for instance, Anthony Beck, Bishop of Durham, commanded 140 knights. Similarly, the earliest naval chaplains did not experience problems in having both spiritual and combatant duties; however, chaplains preferred to use the mace rather than the sword because 'although the Scripture forbade the shedding of blood, there was no restriction on the dashing out of brains.'[2]

With the Reformation and the reduction in the secular power of the church, military chaplains came to be employed in a fashion which is more recognizable to contemporary chaplains. Cromwell's New Model Army, built as much upon spiritual as upon secular principles, had a large number of chaplains attached to individual regiments. The navy of the Napoleonic Wars had chaplains on many ships; their station in action was in the cockpit, where the wounded and dying were taken. One naval chaplain, Alexander John Scott, attended Nelson in his dying moments.

It was during the two World Wars of this century that military chaplaincy developed into the professional ministry it is today. Whilst chaplains would not have been welcome on battlefields, ships and air stations if they were pacifist, in this century chaplains have to be able to minister the gospel to military personnel with full integrity. In the quagmire of the trenches of the Western Front, the need for Christian ministry, like that practised by the Reverend T. B. Hardy (awarded the Victoria Cross for rescuing wounded men from no man's land) was obvious. Similarly when John Collins, chaplain at Bomber Command HQ during the Second World War, had reservations over the policy of area bombing, he did not hesitate to confront the Commander-in-Chief, 'Bomber' Harris.

Although the earliest history of military chaplaincy could be seen to provide ammunition for those who question its validity as a ministry, there is little doubt that subsequent history has demonstrated that, because war is the hardest place, it is the place where chaplains need to be, to provide spiritual care both to the rank and file and to those in command. Put simply, military personnel want to have chaplains around, especially in time of danger and fear. At the turn of the millennium there are chaplains wherever there are military personnel, including in the most remote and dangerous situations; there is even an RAF chaplain on a Royal Naval aircraft carrier!

The role of a military chaplain

We have said that chaplains are there to provide for the spiritual needs of the military community, but what does this mean? In one sense it means providing for military communities the same pastoral and liturgical services as are provided by civilian clergy. Military chaplains conduct services on Sundays and during the week, often in establishment chapels, they baptize, conduct weddings, bury the dead. They also provide pastoral care for all personnel and their families, often dealing with marriage and other welfare problems. Indeed, chaplains require no more skills to perform these functions than any minister will possess, but what they do need is to be an identifiable member of the service community.

The service community has certain characteristics which mark it as being quite different from a civilian community. Because the majority of service personnel retire aged 55 at the latest, the service community is composed of relatively young people, and those who are often far removed from their wider families. As a consequence, at a time when personnel are getting married and having children, the service has to fill the gap left by the absence of parents and siblings. These families are also often, to use an unpopular military expression, 'headless', meaning that the service person within the family is away from home for a high proportion of time. This is especially true with the end of the Cold War and the increased number of 'Out of Area' operations in such places as the Middle East and Bosnia. Additionally, the service community exists within a hierarchical structure where every service person, except the one at the very top, is under someone's command. This means that military personnel not only lack the liberty to go where they want when they want, but also are unable to keep a private life very private.

There is no doubt that the service community feels that it is different from the civilian community, with civilian 'outsiders' viewed with some suspicion ('they do not understand'). It is essential therefore for Christian ministry to military personnel to be provided by chaplains who are fully integrated and identified with the military community. If they were outsiders chaplains would have little effect, for there is little sympathy or patience with someone who does not understand the community, its language, its way of life and its concerns.

It cannot be doubted that the identifiable character of the military chaplain allows for pastoral and liturgical duties to be carried out more effectively (baptisms and marriages are conducted by a recognized member of the community) and that the chaplain can have a wide significance within the community. The chaplain is part of the military team of which a Station or Unit is composed and is there to provide ministry to everyone, churchgoers or not. As a consequence, his duties often take him away from those normally associated with a parish-based minister; he works as a member of a welfare team with doctors, welfare workers and commanders; he often co-ordinates welfare facilities; he has access to the commanding officer and is given the privilege, and right, to comment on the well-being of those under the former's command. The chaplain takes a very incarnational gospel to people; he does not expect them to come to him.

Within all this, there are two very important gifts the chaplains can give the military community. The first is confidentiality. As already noted, in the military community privacy is difficult to maintain; it is understandable that commanders want to know what is going on in the private lives of personnel who may be about to take off in a fast jet loaded with bombs and missiles or to take to the streets of Belfast with a loaded gun. The escape valve for this particular pressure cooker can be the chaplain who is able to offer to personnel complete confidentiality. In this he is trusted by all ranks; he is able to provide the privacy that personnel do not necessarily receive elsewhere. The second gift is the ability to visit both the personnel at work and their families at home; both the 'technical' and the 'domestic' sites are the chaplain's parish and he is in a position to offer that wholeness of ministry which can influence both work and home, often connecting the two. A chaplain may visit a wife at home, her husband in his workplace and the husband's superior officer, in an integrated fashion. Military chaplaincy has been described as the glue which holds the community together and the oil which keeps it working.

Much of that which has been said by way of description of the chaplain's role could be described as fundamentally pastoral; indeed, most military chaplains would see themselves as being involved in about as pastoral a ministry as it is possible to imagine. There are other, no less significant roles, fulfilled by military chaplains. It may be unique that chaplains are allocated time within the training of all trainees to teach beliefs and values. At times this has been 'off the cuff', but in recent years a programme of beliefs and values training has been developed which leads to trainees having to think about some of the most important issues that any human being has to face. When personnel are thrown into situations in which beliefs and values are difficult to keep hold of, the significance of good quality training in this area is as important as their learning how to maintain an aircraft or operate a radar.

Another distinctive role which chaplains have is the ability to speak to those in command and those at the bottom of the military structure. Within the RAF, for instance, a chaplain can take a senior non-commissioned officer to task for his treatment of his people just as the Chaplain-in-Chief can remind members of the Air Force Board of their moral and spiritual duties. Whether they like it or not, those who make decisions about other people and their lives are never far away from the presence of Christ as represented by the chaplain.

War

It is when the military community moves from its peacetime role to the operational environment that military chaplaincy is seen with its full distinctiveness. There are those who would argue that the main role of the chaplain in war is to raise morale and to convince personnel that God is on their side. It is an attitude easy to caricature and was personified by Bishop Winnington-Ingram, Bishop of London during the First World War, who said in a sermon in 1915 'everyone that puts principle above ease, and life itself beyond mere living, are banded in a great crusade – we cannot deny it – to kill Germans: to kill them not for the sake of killing, but to save the world'.[3]

Winnington-Ingram was not a chaplain, but there are those who believe that the task of the chaplain is to justify the use of arms. This is absurd and would be treated with contempt by military personnel, few, if any, of whom have any desire to fire their weapons and kill anyone. It would be wrong, however, to deny that chaplains do have a role in explaining the ethics of operations to personnel and that part of their role in this environment is to work with those who may have troubled consciences. What they do not do is justify the unjustifiable; there have been many examples of chaplains complaining to military commanders about the ethics of the military decisions which are being taken.

In reality, chaplains will rarely be consulted before a military operation about its ethics (although it is interesting to note that the NATO forces do use lawyers to advise on the legality of operations). However, the most valued role of the chaplain in the operational environment is to provide care for those who are frightened, for those who are wounded and for those who are dying and dead. To quote Fr Mulcahy in the television programme *M·A·S·H·*, 'the chaplain brings humanity to an inhumane situation'. When people are frightened, when death is a very real possibility and when people are being wounded, the presence of someone who can provide spiritual comfort is greatly appreciated. As a consequence, in operational environments, personnel who never normally pray will ask the chaplain to pray with and for them, they will attend services of worship, they will talk endlessly to someone who is prepared to listen and understand about their fears and their feelings. However, a chaplain who is not able to look after himself in the operational environment would not be welcome. Perhaps the hard-hearted and cynical would rationalize this chaplaincy presence on the battlefield and say that if he deals with some of the fear the personnel will fight better. The chaplain, however, will regard this role as bringing to personnel the love of God at a time when they are most in need of it. It would be anti-Christian to deny them this reassurance.

Although the chaplain's key role at a time of conflict is with the personnel who are 'in the front line', another important role at such a time is with the families of those who have gone away. During a time of conflict there are many, often quite young, families with one parent/partner away in a dangerous situation. The fear here is quite tangible. The role of the chaplain in this situation is not dissimilar to that of being with those involved in the operations; he will pray, he will talk and he will listen. He will also work to alleviate the boredom and loneliness of those left behind at home by the organization of and attendance at social support groups. Those who are involved at the front line are comforted to know that their families at home, perhaps thousands of miles away, are being looked after by someone who is as trusted as the chaplain.

Military chaplains often say that some of the most difficult, yet rewarding, work they do is at times of conflict, either through involvement with those at the front line or with those at home. Never is the need for Christian ministry more urgent than during these times.

Role tensions

To return to the beginning; war is the 'hardest' place, and it would be wrong to deny that, because of the ethical complexity of military life and operations around this hardest place, the military chaplain can find his role and integrity compromised. The most obvious example is the possible incongruity between the Christian basis of a chaplain's ministry and the patently un-Christian situations in which he finds himself. If Christianity requires pacifism, as some would affirm, then the notion of Christian chaplains is unsustainable. This is an important point for any chaplain to address, not only for himself but also for the often very committed Christians within the Armed Forces to whom he ministers. This issue cannot be avoided and a chaplain will be frequently called upon to address it. We cannot know whether Christ was a pacifist or not, although those who work in military chaplaincy will have been required to reach some conclusion. The position usually taken by chaplains is that war is evil but that there are times when it is the lesser of two evils (according to the 'Just War' theory) and that the Christian church exists in a world which is essentially, 'between the times', between the Incarnation and the realization of the Kingdom of God. During this time war, as ethically controlled as possible, may be seen to be necessary to relieve the suffering of the weak and to limit the oppression of the powerful.

Another area where it is possible for a chaplain's ministerial integrity to be compromised is connected to the way in which the British Chaplaincy Services are organized. In the British Armed Forces, someone who becomes a chaplain, whilst still sponsored by the church, ceases to be an employee of the church. If the notion is accepted that an employee will always meet the requirements of his employer before anything else, then there is a possibility for chaplains to place their commanders in a higher position perhaps than God. This may be particularly the case where chaplains wear rank (as in the Army and the RAF). Add to this the perception that commanders would rather chaplains adhere to a pastoral model of ministry (that is, an ordained welfare worker) than to a prophetic model, then it can be seen that the chaplain has to be very strong and in possession of a clear vision to maintain integrity.

There is no doubt that such a situation does create a tension. A commander is not always keen to have a prophetic chaplain continually 'poking his chest'. He would much rather the chaplain kept quiet and looked after the welfare of the community. Most chaplains, however, would not be content to accept the will of the commander on this matter. Most would see it as their responsibility, convenient or not, to speak the truth prophetically to their commanders whatever the consequences. This does require strength of will and confidence but can often be managed if the chaplain has developed a close enough relationship with his commander and is thus able to speak out without fear.

The fact that army and air force chaplains wear rank can also lead to a possibility of a chaplain's ministry being compromised. A chaplain's rank, where he has it, is always relative; it is an honorary rank which is subordinate to his ecclesiastical title. A rank's use is in being able to speak confidently within a hierarchy in which rank is predominant. The drawbacks are that a senior officer can 'pull rank', whilst junior ranks may be put off from approaching a chaplain who is a senior officer. Most chaplains however are able to wear the rank in a way which enables them to operate efficiently in a hierarchical organization without distancing themselves from those for whom they have pastoral care. As with any minister, the chaplain's success in doing this is dependent upon his personality. It is interesting to note that in the Navy chaplains do not wear (or indeed receive) rank but asssume the rank of the person with whom they are talking, be it admiral or rating.

One of the most difficult experiences chaplains have is connected to this wearing of rank but has nothing to do with the military environment. Chaplains wearing uniform are often treated with suspicion by their civilian colleagues, some of whom tend to assume that military chaplains have 'sold out' to the military organization and have allowed their ministry to be compromised. Chaplains might thus be looked upon as 'establishment people' who adhere to right-wing politics. A consequence of this is that military chaplains can find it difficult to gain employment after their military service. It is, in fact, a misinformed attitude. Because chaplains have been faced with ministry in very difficult and demanding situations where they have often had to challenge authority, they tend to be thoughtful people and critical of the status quo. Whilst there is a tendency to conservatism of attitude, there is certainly no tendency to blind acceptance of misguided authority.

Theological issues

Although there may be some expectation, especially by those of the most senior rank, and even more by those who have retired from a military career, that chaplains should provide safe institutionalized and establishment religion, contemporary chaplains do not tend to be particularly conservative, either liturgically or theologically. The theology of incarnation continually demands attention from the chaplain. He spends a relatively short time in the week nourishing an often small community of worshipping Christians. Chaplains spend much more time taking the gospel, taking Christ, out into barracks, into hangars, on to ships; following Christ by incarnating God in the places where people are, reminding them of God's presence. In doing so the chaplain looks beyond traditional church activity, which appeals to few people, and both attempts to make those activities more relevant and meaningful to secular military personnel and to find other ways of conveying Christian teaching to these people. Here beliefs and values training, well delivered, is so valuable. Because of this theological insight military chaplains will throw themselves into the organization of welfare facilities which perhaps have little or nothing to do with church activities.

We have already noted the prophetic aspect of a military chaplain's ministry but, as well as being able to be the thorn in the flesh of the military hierarchy, the chaplain is also its servant. Despite the fact that the chaplain may be dressed in uniform with a rank, he is often in a position of getting alongside the people with whom he is working. A chaplain would not be carrying out his full ministry if he did not immerse himself in the life of the community. As a consequence, he will go on exercise with his unit, take the basic fitness test, undergo nuclear, biological and chemical training. The chaplain will be, should be, the one who helps along the weaker personnel, forgetting his own needs in order to support others.

This incarnational gospel the military chaplain preaches is also pragmatic and, in some sense, secular. Very few people will come to chaplains looking for God in any conventional sense. Instead, chaplains have to go to the personnel and find God in them, often giving expression in very secular terms. Within this situation there is great freedom, for the many exhausting and preoccupying demands of running a worshipping community can be set to one side and energy can be diverted into looking at ways in which God can be made more relevant and immanent.

Conclusion

Within the military community chaplains are an accepted part of the landscape who maintain credibility by being where personnel are and by being fully involved in the life of the unit. The gospel is present throughout military establishments with chaplains constantly seeking to make it relevant and meaningful. There may be times when the chaplain's position as a military person might dominate his position as a minister but it is in this tension that the most effective witness can be carried out. Through his presence in operational and other military environments, the chaplain takes Christ to the place where he is urgently needed and through that experience is able to assist personnel in developing a Christ-centred relationship. Perhaps the church has something to learn from its ministers who work in such places.

Notes

1   Michael Walzer, *Just and Unjust Wars* (London: Allen Lane, 1977), p. xvii.
2   Gordon Taylor, *The Sea Chaplains* (Oxford: Blackwell, 1977), p. 2.
3   Alan Wilkinson, *The Church of England in the First World War* (London: SPCK, 1978), p. 217.

7

Arts and recreation

William Hall and Robert Cooper

Introduction

The Chaplaincy to the Arts and Recreation in North-East England was formed in 1968. Currently it has a team of four chaplains, who work regionally in the dioceses of York, Durham and Newcastle. The chaplaincy exists to enable the churches in this region to be more effective in relating their ministry and mission to the cultural life of the community.

The chaplaincy's aims

The chaplaincy organizes its work around four aims. The first of these is:

To develop a prophetic and pastoral ministry which recognizes and affirms the importance of creativity and recreativity for individuals and society.

Over the years the chaplaincy has developed an understanding of 'creativity' and 'recreativity' which underpins its work. The human ability to create is God's gift and through it he calls people to join him in bringing joy and fulfilment to the earth and all its creatures. Such creativity is not the exclusive preserve of the artist, though the chaplaincy's work focuses on this mode of its expression. All forms of creativity share in the power to re-create. Whether we make music or listen to it, watch football or play it, the experience can be renewing. Theologically, Christians understand this as Christ fulfilling his promise to give us life – and to give it more abundantly.

In his book *The Empty Space* theatre director Peter Brook offers another perspective on this link between creativity and spirituality. His concern is the theatre, but he could well be writing about all the arts, when he says 'Many audiences all over the world will answer positively from their own experience that they have seen the face of the invisible through an experience on the stage that transcended their experience in life'.[1] When Brook claims that theatre has the power to reveal 'the invisible' and 'the transcendent', he is using religious language. This should not surprise us. God's Holy Spirit is active in all human communities – opening 'eyes that are closed, hearts that are unaware and minds that shrink from too much reality', as Bishop John V. Taylor has put it.[2]

A great theatre director writing about the arts and a Christian thinker describing the work of the Holy Spirit are clearly saying something very similar. Both picture light coming into dark places. Both sense the possibility of new beginnings. Throughout its work the chaplaincy supports and encourages this natural alliance between Christianity and the arts. But how does it give practical expression to this theological understanding? What follows in the rest of this chapter can only give a small flavour of the many projects which have taken place over the last thirty years.

One of the most important has been the establishment and administration of a residency for an artist at Durham cathedral. To accomplish this the chaplaincy has developed a partnership which exemplifies its policy of achieving its aims through working collaboratively with other bodies, both secular and religious. Created in 1983, the residency's aim has been to support an artist at a critical stage in the development of his or her work. Amongst artists, this opportunity is now one of the most sought-after in the UK. Those who hold the residency are encouraged to respond to the rich artistic tradition that surrounds them, of which Durham cathedral is clearly the most profound aspect. The basis of the residency is a dialogue between the artist and this challenging situation, which leads to renewed vision and inspiration. Through the residency the chaplaincy is witnessing to the value of the arts in human existence and challenging both church and community to recognize them as God's gifts.

Another major project occurred during 1996, the UK Year of the Visual Arts, which was hosted by the northern region. As part of its contribution the chaplaincy commissioned acclaimed American video artist Bill Viola to carry out a work for Durham cathedral. His response was *The Messenger*. In this work a waterbound figure rises from the depths to emerge and take a breath of life, before sinking back beneath the surface. The cycle is repeated five times over a 25-minute period. The work explores profound themes of life, death and human becoming. Though not intentionally Christian, it was a site-specific piece, to be placed by the cathedral font, which gave it deep resonances of baptism and new life. Having seen it, a reviewer for *The Guardian* newspaper wrote that Bill Viola 'remains one of the very few Western contemporary artists capable of embodying a convincing sense of spirituality' (2 August 1997).

This project achieved many things, including bringing a new audience into contact with contemporary art and a new audience into the cathedral. Though the nakedness of the figure in *The Messenger* caused controversy, it created many openings for exploring the issues it raised with students, churchpeople and members of the public. On television and in the press, in letters and in private discussion, the opportunity arose to speak about the quest for what it means to be truly human – and of other aspects of the common ground between the arts and the church.

Pastoral ministry is part and parcel of such projects. As any Christian in such a situation, the chaplains respond as representatives of God's church. Their experience of work in the arts, however, can valuably inform this aspect of their ministry. It may also be that the seriousness with which the chaplains have taken an individual artist's work, or the affirmation they have offered in the past, will mean that their pastoral ministry is more readily welcomed. Friendship and trust do not need to be established first – they have already been made.

Many of these pastoral contacts are passing and informal, whilst others are officially recognized and licensed, such as the chaplaincy to Middlesbrough Football Club, which was held by one of our team for over twenty years. Similar pastoral work continues with the Northern Section of the Showmen's Guild of Great Britain. Moving from fairground to fairground, showmen are often unable to maintain contact with a local church. In this setting the chaplain becomes the church's official representative and this leads to many occasional offices and to other pastoral work such as visiting the sick or elderly. However, this is not an individual ministry. Here, too, the chaplains seek to build partnerships, involving local clergy wherever possible, so as to strengthen links between showmen's families and local churches.

Strong pastoral links also exist with people in the performing arts, especially through the Actors' Church Union (ACU). In various ways ACU chaplains demonstrate the care and concern of the church for those on stage, backstage and front-of-house. The chaplaincy's senior chaplain is currently also Senior Chaplain of the ACU; part of this role is to arrange the appointment of some 200 chaplains to theatres, film and television studios.

From time to time pastoral ministry demands that the chaplaincy addresses larger issues which are affecting the lives of individuals or communities. Such a concern lay behind the conference 'A Serious Business', through which people in the performing arts met with ACU chaplains to listen to speakers such as Jeremy Isaacs and Timothy West and debated the future of the theatre. In a similar way, the trust that has been built up over the years through pastoral work with the Showmen's Guild has led to other kinds of involvement in their lives. The chaplaincy has, for example, helped on occasions in negotiations with local authorities about the siting of fairs.

The chaplaincy's second aim is:

To explore and witness to the human capacity for creative and recreative activity as a way of expressing life and seeking its purpose.

Over the years, perhaps the chaplaincy's primary response to this aim has been IMPASSE. Its origins lie in the late 1960s, when Teesside's heavy industries were in decline and it was clear that unemployment on a vast scale was here to stay.

The negative implications of this situation for human creativity were immense. The chaplaincy's first initiative was therefore to establish exactly what those implications were by listening to people without paid employment. It was they who were largely responsible for identifying six basic human needs:

- the opportunity to make a positive contribution to the community
- a sense of personal identity and self-worth
- friendship
- the chance to realize creative potential
- a rhythm of life
- money – for safety, security and survival.

What also became clear was that society was so organized that people had become accustomed to these needs being met largely through paid work. Those for whom paid work was an increasingly unlikely prospect therefore faced needs far wider than a lack of cash. The chaplaincy worked with them to develop ways in which life could have purpose and meaning with or without paid employment. The name given to the enterprise was IMPASSE – an ironic name. In society we seemed to have reached an impasse. Nationally, politicians seemed to have no answers, but locally, people were prepared to try a possible new way forward.

IMPASSE remains a philosophy, rather than a programme. It adopts a bi-focal approach. It accepts that, in the short term, individuals have personal needs for fulfilment and creative growth which must be addressed, but it also recognizes the need for long-term change. Society itself has to be challenged to find new patterns of living in community, which enable people to realize their full potential, whether or not they have paid employment. For over twenty years, from bases across the North-East (with one also in Scotland), the IMPASSE philosophy took tangible form. Primary figures in the partnership which made this possible were, first and foremost, those without paid employment themselves, but other individuals and organizations were drawn together in the exploration: local councillors; local authority officers; Councils of

Churches; representatives of the voluntary sector; those responsible for government training schemes.

Though there were IMPASSE buildings containing well-equipped work-
shops, they were not ends in themselves. They were not centres for the
unemployed, but bases from which the work and philosophy could move out
into the community. IMPASSE released resources and the resources released
people. One special example was Chris and Stuart Newman, two brothers who
built a catamaran at IMPASSE Middlesbrough. They then learnt navigation
and sailed in it to the West Indies. For them this was not only a personal
challenge, but a symbol of all that people without paid employment could
achieve.

A less spectacular, but equally profound example, was Kit. So depressed
by unemployment that he had almost to be pushed there by his wife, Kit found
his way into the woodwork shop. A redundant steelworker, he found he had a
natural aptitude with wood. Soon he was turning out furniture to the extent
that Social Security officers questioned whether he was operating a small
industry! He was able to prove that all his work was either for personal use or
as gifts for people like his daughter, who was setting up home. In relating the
experience, this is how he explained his true motivation:

> Before I came to IMPASSE I didn't want to get up in the morning. Now I
> can't wait to get in, I have so much to do and so many people to see. I'm so
> excited, too, because I feel as if I've been wasting my life on metal, a dead
> thing, now that I've discovered what I can do with wood – a living material.
> My skills are even saving me money and, what's more, they have given me
> a new, respected place in the community. People come to me for help.[3]

Without knowing it, he had expressed the six basic needs which discussions
had identified years before – and how they were being met through IMPASSE.

New ways to pursue the IMPASSE philosophy are now being explored,
most recently through the appointment of a chaplaincy-sponsored research
student at Durham University. He is working with the team in investigating
the rationale needed to commend IMPASSE more widely.

The chaplaincy's third aim is:

*To encourage an awareness of, and a Christian response to, issues concerning the
Church, arts and recreation.*

It cannot be stressed strongly enough that, at every point, the chaplaincy seeks
to relate what it is doing to the parishes and to work in partnership with them.
'Art in Northern Churches' is an example of this. Through this scheme,
challenging, contemporary work is placed in churches and a dialogue initiated

between local people and the artists. Over a period of six months, eight parishes were enabled to display 16 works by leading painters Mark Cazalet and Richard Kenton Webb. The paintings were moved around between the churches, remaining long enough for parishioners to have the experience of living with them over a worthwhile period. Through meetings with the artists and a final gallery show, church people and visitors were given the opportunity to explore issues which arise from the making of contemporary art. They also gained a new and deeper insight into the creative process itself. Both painters also spoke of the value they placed on the experience. Responding to the challenges expressed by people meant that both had developed their approach to their work.

The chaplaincy also played its part locally in bringing the social, economic and cultural issues facing the nation in the 1997 General Election into clearer focus. These issues became the subject of a programme of events entitled 'The Futures We Can Choose'. This series of lectures and discussions, organized by the Churches Regional Commission in the North-East, grew from an idea put forward by the chaplaincy. Such topics as 'The Future of the Justice System' or 'Education' and 'The Arts' were introduced by a leading speaker, who was responded to by a theologian. Discussion then followed amongst an audience which included people from all walks of life, secular and religious. The chaplaincy participated in planning and organizing the initial series and is contributing to the others which have grown from it.

Because of its wide experience and long-standing involvement in the arts, the chaplaincy's advice is also frequently sought, for example, by churches and cathedrals considering the installation of works of art or appropriate artists to carry them out. Advice is also sought by arts practitioners and many students of all art forms. In addition, chaplains finds themselves drawn into such things as the development of a local government cultural policy and sitting on the management committees of arts organizations.

Over the years the chaplaincy's work has also required it to get to grips with a wide variety of government legislation. From our vantage point, we have been able to advise bishops and others on matters as varied as the Gaming Act, the Licensing Laws, the National Lottery, the Broadcasting Act, cross-media ownership and certain types of entertainment such as stage hypnotism.

The chaplaincy's fourth aim is:

To stimulate and encourage theological exploration of the concept of creativity and recreativity.

As part of its practice, the chaplaincy has regularly organized conferences to explore aspects of the relationship between the church and the arts. 'Art and the Spiritual', for example, marked the installation of Bill Viola's *The Messenger* in Durham cathedral in 1996. The form of the conference enabled arts practitioners such as film producer David Puttnam, *Angel of the North* sculptor Antony Gormley, as well as Bill Viola himself, to engage in debate with leading theologians. It successfully brought together members of the churches and the arts community to explore common concerns.

This conference took its form from an earlier consultation between artists and theologians which the chaplaincy had been promoting for some years. The chaplaincy believes that its theological purpose is best served by building bridges which reach towards those outside as well as those inside the church. The chaplaincy's work constantly brings it into contact with people who, without necessarily professing any faith, are clearly on a similar journey. Someone who expressed this convergence, but from the opposite perspective, was an art critic, the late Peter Fuller. He wrote: 'Incorrigible atheist and aesthete that I am, I believe it to be a moot point whether art can ever thrive outside that sort of living, symbolic order, with deep tendrils in communal life, which, it seems, a flourishing religion alone can provide.'[4]

The many partnerships which sustain the chaplaincy's work are testimony to this mutually sustaining relationship between faith and the arts. It is not only the chaplaincy which values these partnerships; invitations such as that extended by celebratory theatre company Welfare State International to chair a conference which they were arranging concerning funerals, indicate that there is a much wider appreciation of the partnership developed. Organized for artists, the aim of the conference was to encourage participants to make their special contribution to helping people through the grieving process. The chaplaincy's participation in the event continued a long-standing relationship.

Conclusion

Sometimes the chaplaincy's central concerns come together and find exhilarating expression in a single event, such as 'Duke Ellington in Durham Cathedral'. Many people are unaware that Duke Ellington was a committed Christian. Towards the end of his life he sought to express his faith in a series of 'Sacred Concerts'. Taking the great symphonic masses as a model, one of the chaplaincy team ordered elements of these 'Sacred Concerts' as a setting for the Mass. The music was arranged by the internationally acclaimed jazz pianist and composer Stan Tracey, a noted Ellington interpreter, and the Stan Tracey Orchestra performed the Duke Ellington 'Mass' with soloists, dancers and the cathedral choir. Strikingly, it was an academic expert on Victorian hymnody who commented 'The first time I found the Ellington "Mass" extraordinarily exciting, so I expected the second time to be a disappointment. In fact, it was less exciting, but deeply satisfying spiritually. The integration of the music and the Mass was what particularly struck me on the second occasion.'[5]

In the Duke Ellington 'Mass', human creativity was celebrated in the work of the performers and those who led the worship. The congregation went away renewed and refreshed – re-created, we could say. It was an extraordinary experience, but it was only possible within the context of celebrating, in the Eucharist, the divine creativity of the cross and the renewing, re-creative power of the resurrection. Here, as in everything, God – creator and redeemer – remains both the inspiration of and justification for the chaplaincy's work.

Notes

1   Peter Brook, *The Empty Space* (Harmondsworth: Penguin, 1990), p. 48.
2   John V. Taylor, *The Go-Between God* (London: SCM Press, 1972), p. 19.
3   Quoted in Bill Hall, 'IMPASSE: a possible way forward', *Northern Economic Review*, no. 22 (Autumn 1994).
4   Peter Fuller, *Images of God* (London: Hogarth Press, 1990), p. 189.
5   Professor Richard Watson, quoted by Jon Williams, 'Cherished ambitions', *Choir and Organ* (April/May 1995), p. 27.

8

Hospitals

Georgina Nelson

Historical overview

'I was sick, and ye visited me.' Visitors to the Royal Infirmary of Edinburgh still pass beneath these words from St Matthew's Gospel, carved in the stonework above the main entrance. They form the 'charter and inspiration' of the service of the hospital chaplain.[1]

From the beginning of the Christian era, great importance has been accorded to the task of ministry to the sick. In this way could the example and command of Christ himself be followed, by those who sought to honour and serve him in the person of the afflicted. Special buildings to house the sick were erected in various parts of the Roman Empire; references to hospitals in Gaul can be found as early as the fifth century.

In the mediaeval period, most monasteries cared for the sick, notably for lepers, and many modern hospitals in the UK are descendants of mediaeval monastic institutions. Although the administration of these places of healing had largely been transferred into lay hands by the time of the Reformation, the activities of parish clergy in visiting the sick still testified to the historic connection between religion, health and healing.

The practice of appointing a member of the clergy specifically to look after the religious needs of patients was known in England in the seventeenth century, and had become widespread by the nineteenth. When the great infirmaries developed in Scotland in the eighteenth century there was chaplaincy provision; for example, the Royal Infirmary of Edinburgh acquired a chaplain in 1755, whose official status was underscored by the fact that his duties required him to open with prayer the meetings of the board of management.

With the advent of the National Health Service in 1948, hospital authorities were advised that they should make provision for meeting spiritual need, and that one or more chaplains should be appointed, in consultation with the appropriate church authorities. The ensuing years saw an increase in the number of chaplains appointed.

Current trends

Considerable uncertainty regarding the fate of chaplaincy greeted the reorganization of the NHS in the early 1990s. The publication in 1992 of the NHS Executive Guidelines on *Meeting the Spiritual Needs of Patients and Staff* seemed however to reaffirm the position of chaplaincy, advising that employing authorities should 'make every effort to provide for the spiritual needs of patients and staff'. Recent statistics suggest that health-care managers are recognizing the value of chaplaincy; the years 1994–96 saw an increase of 77 in the number of whole-time chaplains in post, and data from July 1997 indicate that there are currently some 350 whole-time chaplains and chaplain's assistants in post in the UK. The chief executive of the Hospital Chaplaincies' Council has remarked recently that 'NHS chaplains are better represented and funded now than at any point in the past 25 years'.[2]

The years around the millennium constitute a period of challenge and of change for chaplains, with elements both of insecurity and of creativity. In response to the new business ethos of the NHS, some chaplaincies are being required to become budget holders, to produce business plans, to become involved in audit and quality initiatives and to take on a wider remit within the hospital (for example in co-ordinating bereavement care or volunteer services). The challenge posed by such developments has been eagerly taken up by some chaplaincy departments, and yet many chaplains feel a certain unease at the prospect of translating their work into the language of business, fearing that something of the non-measurable human aspect might be devalued in the process. All chaplains none the less are encouraged to adopt a more structured, professional approach to their tasks than hitherto, and in this they have been assisted by the publication in 1993 of Health Care Chaplaincy Standards. Chaplains are also encouraged to participate in some of the increasing variety of in-service training courses which are available. In addition, there is a need to find ways of functioning effectively within an increasingly multi-faith environment, in order to meet the spiritual needs of all; chaplaincies have in some cases become multi-faith teams, consisting of whole and part-time, male and female, non-Christian and Christian chaplains working together with a sense of shared responsibility for all. That responsibility is increasingly being exercised towards hospital staff, many of whom are suffering the stressful effects of rapid change, and who need the support of those who are seen to be outside the structures of management.

The role of the chaplain continues to be reshaped in response to current trends. The fundamental challenge remains that of exercising, in a bewildering and rapidly changing situation, the pastoral care which is in essence 'to help people to know love, both as something to be received and as something to give'.[3]

The role of the chaplain

Prophet, priest, administrator, counsellor, teacher, evangelist, judge, servant, healer, friend . . .[4]

Ethicist, patients' advocate, psychotherapist, resident theologian, adviser to the ward team, enabler and teacher, an interpreter who functions and communicates at the interface between science and religion, the hospital and the church.[5]

The hospital chaplain will take up and leave aside many roles, and must in some respects be a chameleon-like figure. Who he is will depend, among other things, upon the type of hospital, the particular situation and the expectations of those involved, the denomination or faith group to which he belongs and his own personal style and gifts. In addition, his role will be nuanced according to whether he is whole or part-time, and whether he sees his responsibility as being principally for those of his own faith group. Underpinning all else, and holding together the multiplicity of roles which may fall to the chaplain, there is the chaplain's most basic calling: to be, to be present, to be himself – the same self both professionally and personally, with the integrity which has the potential to free others to be, to be present, to be themselves.

The chaplain and spiritual care

Every person is a spiritual being, having a spiritual dimension, and thus spiritual need is universal.[6]

Understood thus, spiritual care is not an optional extra, to be provided for those who are actively religious; it becomes an integral part of the holistic approach which is held up as an ideal in modern health care, and it has relevance to all.

Spiritual need, understood broadly as the search for meaning, may find expression in the 'why?' questions which are commonly asked in the context of illness, and which give voice to anxiety, anger, guilt, loneliness and other such difficult emotions. Such questions may express a need for acceptance, hope, forgiveness and love.

A narrow understanding of spiritual need as religious need pure and simple gives the chaplain well–defined tasks to perform, tasks which are uniquely his. It also identifies a particular constituency of patients who are the chaplain's special concern, i.e. those requiring the offices of the church. The role of the chaplain can thus be easily understood by hospital staff. However, the broader understanding of spiritual need as described above, while positive and interesting in itself, and widely welcomed by most chaplains, nevertheless means that the chaplain's role has become more diffuse and more difficult to define, having to do with so many diverse expressions of the pain (and joy) of the human condition. Whilst the chaplain can only welcome a recognition of his relevance as a resource for all, not just for the religious few, he may find himself at times in polite competition with psychologists, counsellors and other therapists who may regard themselves as being generally the appropriate professionals to meet expressions of spiritual/psychosocial/emotional need. In the absence of a need which is expressed in overtly religious language, and faced with the poverty of language itself to express such need, it is no easy matter for staff to discern when it is appropriate to call in the chaplain.

Taking these circumstances into account who, for patients and staff, does the chaplain need to be?

(1) The chaplain as listener.

He needs to be one who listens. Hopefully he is not burdened with any too–precise definitions of how spiritual need might manifest itself, nor with any easy theories as to how it might be met. Whilst he may well have some training in 'listening skills', he is aware that there is a kind of listening, a quality of human communication which cannot be taught, but which can only arise out of who we are and what we have made of life. Listening, in this sense, is part of loving. It is open to hear those things which will not arrive clothed in the language of the church, nor are likely to be stated bluntly. The chaplain listens for those metaphors which hint at the truth of how a person perceives his situation; for the throwaway line which tells all. He does this in the setting of the hospital, in which precision of scientific vocabulary and lucidity of scientific explanation sweep (almost) all before them.

(2) One who supports and affirms staff in their own caring.

Many staff feel ill-equipped by training or temperament to venture into the realms of spiritual care. The chaplain can be supportive, and may convey to staff that the sensitive carer who is able to respond with simple human warmth can play an invaluable role in meeting spiritual needs. In this role the chaplain may be welcomed not so much as another 'expert' in his field, but as someone who affirms others in the human skills which they may have learned to mistrust or devalue in favour of training or technique.

The chaplain: amateur or professional?

The chaplain who ministers daily to 'religious' and 'non-religious' alike quickly sets aside those tendencies to categorize which can be so prevalent within the hospital, as elsewhere. He himself defies categorization. The hospital is a setting in which professionals (health care staff) and amateurs (patients, relatives) are clearly demarcated, and yet the chaplain is both professional and amateur. Like the professional, he has his codes of practice, his education and training. He will have the habit of disciplined reflection upon his effectiveness, and will pay attention to his ongoing development. Unlike the professional, he will have no neat role or clearly defined boundaries, no air of busy-ness to hide behind. He will not wield the power of 'the expert', to whom others look for solutions or for answers. He will not be immune to feelings of powerlessness or failure. His ministry will not have to do with superiority of knowledge, applied to the solving of problems – for life, with its pains, contradictions, its desert places and sudden blossomings, can never be reduced to the dimensions of a problem to be solved. Life makes amateurs of us all.

The chaplain, the sick and the healthy

Likewise, in the hospital setting, human beings are readily categorized into the sick and the healthy. It is easy for the chaplain to collude with this; easy, especially under pressure of role uncertainty, to become yet another therapist, armed with theories and techniques for the solving of 'spiritual problems'.

But the chaplain's approach is not conditioned by the received categories of sickness and health. He is not involved with 'the sick'; his concern is with all, both 'sick' and 'healthy', and he approaches both with the same openness to give and to receive, to teach and to learn, to care and to be cared for. He does not attempt to fit people into any theory, but is open to the uniqueness, unpredictability and sheer elusiveness of persons. He is not in the curing business; his role is to care, to nurture, to affirm others in their strength and giftedness. He also has a concern beyond individuals in isolation, understanding that true health involves persons-in-relation.

Brokenness and wholeness

The chaplain works not so much with the division into healthy and sick individuals, as with the theological categories of brokenness and wholeness, recognizing that the lives of all of us contain elements of both. This understanding allows for the possibility that suffering might, in certain circumstances, be seen not as something to be 'treated' but as integral to growth towards wholeness and depth of personhood. This is part of what Elizabeth Barrett Browning calls 'the broad life-wound', not to be hastily closed up, but to be acknowledged and explored, and in some measure shared.

This same perspective will likewise make it possible to understand death not as defeat, pure and simple, as implied by the medical model of health, but as containing within itself elements of both the brokenness and wholeness of the human condition, both defeat and victory, both destruction of meaning and provision of meaning.

The chaplain and the hospital

The chaplain represents many things to many people within the hospital: a particular church, congregation or faith group; certain values and attitudes; the love, the forgiveness of God; the hope of a life to come and so on. He may also bear witness to certain things within the life of the hospital itself, and be called to minister to the spiritual needs of the hospital as an institution, as well as to those of individuals.

In a setting in which there can be much fragmentation, the chaplain stands for the truth that human beings are more than the sum of their parts. In a context in which technological innovation threatens to sweep all before it, the chaplain is a living reminder of those human qualities of care and nurture which lie at the heart of all healing. In the face of the tendency to medicalize more and more areas of human experience, he also affirms that there is an anguish which is sometimes necessary to human persons, and which is part of life as a responsible agent in a world of strangeness and contradiction.

The chaplain strives to keep the institution warm and human, and to recall it to its task as a community in which true healing is possible. This concerns its values, priorities, ethical decisions, staff relations and attitudes to vulnerable groups. The chaplain is privileged in having access to all, at all levels. He can be priest or prophet, and can recognize the elements of brokenness and wholeness which exist in the lives of institutions as well as of persons. In the face of institutional complacency or fundamentalism, he may stand for the kind of brokenness which challenges all human systems, all human attempts to make life neat, controllable and manageable.

The chaplain and the church

> To be rational in the modern world meant to be a pilgrim and to live out one's life as a pilgrimage. To be rational in the post-modern world means to be a vagrant or a tourist, or to act as one.[7]

Bauman's pilgrim lives a life which he recognizes as having direction, coherence, purpose and a goal. He knows what he believes, and where he belongs. The vagrant, on the other hand, is one who travels on with little sense of ultimate direction or overarching purpose. He stops over temporarily, setting destinations as he goes along. He is insecure in his world, belonging everywhere and nowhere, unsure even of who he is.

It may still be possible in a parish setting, especially if the ministry exercised there focuses largely on the Christian congregation, to minister mostly to pilgrims – to those who have a strong sense of belonging within the church, with an understanding of its language, ritual and tradition. In such a setting the minister will be accorded a certain status, identity, influence and security in his role. The hospital chaplain is accorded none of these by right. He ministers in the postmodern setting of a secular institution, and those who are his chief concern share many of the characteristics of Bauman's vagrant. Here are women and men, both staff and patients, whose goals are short term, perhaps because of illness, or job insecurity. For the most part they have no overarching sense of purpose or belonging or belief, and often no great sense of who they are, beyond the role that they must play. They have learned to adapt, to accept change as the norm. They are only passing through, but without the pilgrim's eye for the distant destination. The language, ritual, structures, beliefs of the church generally mean little or nothing to them. As a result, the chaplain, unlike his colleagues in the parish trained in proclamation, learns to be silent, and to listen with the humility proper to one who has no power, no status.

With that listening posture comes a readiness to learn the language in which the postmodern vagrant expresses his deepest joys and fears and yearnings – not the language of the church, but the language of the everyday – which can convey with impressive simplicity the reality of God, recognized or unrecognized, in the lives of people who are and will remain strangers to the church as an institution.

The chaplain listens. Such spiritual care as he is able to offer will be offered freely, with no ulterior motive, not even that of bringing people 'into the church'. Hospital chaplains are well placed to see that the kingdom is already present, in the care, the honesty, the humour, the courage of those who are brought together in the strange fellowship of the hospital.

Chaplains not infrequently feel that they have moved from the centre to the periphery of the life of the church. This is unfortunate in one sense, but at least provides a perspective from which the life of the church can be seen for what it so often is. There is much exclusiveness in the life of the church. There is a fear of those outside, an ungenerous spirit towards those who are different. There can be a jealous guarding of the sacraments, lest they be unworthily received by those who do not belong. Often 'church' and 'world' are too easily and glibly categorized. For all that we talk about freedom in Christ, it is too often the case that church people feel a singular lack of freedom – freedom to admit to fear, or weakness, or doubt, or need, or anger, or the truth of who they really are. The armour of the Lord can become a defence against our very humanity. Perhaps hospital chaplains can say something to the church, on the basis of their experience. It is the chaplain's experience, living as he does amid the raw and real emotions released within a hospital, that the things that divide us from each other lose all meaning in such a setting; that human beings, admitting to their weakness and vulnerability, can discover together a new wholeness, a way of living with an acceptance of the loose ends, unanswered questions, half-articulated yearnings in life. There can be a searing honesty, a newly sensitive appreciation of the beauty, tragedy and complexity of what it means to be human. In contrast, how small, how careful, how self-regarding the life of the church can seem at times. But Christ, whose ongoing life is forged amid the realities of love and loss, of hope and despair, of forsakenness and deliverance, is more generous than his church, and belongs to all the world, in the solidarity of human experience. Perhaps the witness of hospital chaplaincy can help the church to learn afresh the truth of what it means to lose its life, in order to find it once again.

Notes

1 T. B. Stewart Thompson, *The Chaplain in the Church of Scotland* (Edinburgh: Blackwood, 1947).
2 A. Dix, 'Is God good value?', *Health Service Journal* (11 July 1996), pp. 24–7.
3 Alastair Campbell, *Professionalism and Pastoral Care* (Philadelphia: Fortress, 1995).
4 M. Wilson, *The Hospital – A Place of Truth* (Birmingham: University of Birmingham Institute for the Study of Worship and Religious Architecture, 1971).
5 T. S. McGregor, 'Hospital chaplaincy' in Alastair Campbell, *A Dictionary of Pastoral Care* (London: SPCK, 1987).
6 D. J. Stoter, *Spiritual Aspects of Health Care* (London: Mosby, 1995).
7 Z. Bauman, 'Morality in the age of contingency' in P. Heelas, S. Lash and P. Morris (eds), *Detraditionalisation* (Oxford: Blackwell, 1996).

9

Industry

Denis Claringbull

'We don't want your bloody sort round here!'

This was my first encounter as a raw, young industrial chaplain with a real live shop steward. The meeting took place in a factory in Croydon in 1962. I stood still and said nothing, as a further torrent of abuse emerged from his mouth. I then asked him why he felt so strongly and the reasons emerged: he had had some very bad experiences of 'Vicars' and therefore felt alienated from the church. He had come to identify the church with a bosses' organization and I understood how he felt. Over time we gradually became firm friends and when I eventually left Croydon eight years later he presented me with one of his paintings; for as well as being a skilled engineer, he was a talented artist.

The alienation of many working people from the churches was one of the principal reasons for the emergence of industrial mission as a sector ministry. One of the founding fathers of industrial mission, the Revd Ted Wickham (later Bishop of Middleton), wrote of the historic alienation of the English working classes and the church. He wrote that the Church of England had not lost the working classes, but that it had never had them.[1] The system of pew rents in the established church was a strong disincentive to working people to attend church, which was a largely middle-class institution. Other denominations, to a lesser extent, had similar problems. The roots of industrial mission in Britain, as an attempt to counter this alienation, can be traced back to the Navvy Mission to the constructors of the railways at the beginning of the nineteenth century. It was a mission to evangelize an alienated and tough workforce.

However alienation was not the only reason for the churches' involvement in ministry in people's place of work. Churches of all denominations have

83

become increasingly congregational over the last hundred years; increasingly concerned with internal and domestic affairs, rather than with wider concerns which affect the general quality of life. The church has, at its best, always cared about the whole of creation and not just local, particular concerns. Because industry has a profound influence on all of human life and on the rest of the created world, the church cannot afford to ignore it. In terms of mission, the church knows that it cannot remain peripheral to secular society. The Church of England (and established churches in other countries too) has a parochial system which embraces the whole of society (although this responsibility and opportunity can so easily be forgotten). Industrial mission arose to bridge the gap which had emerged between industry and the church.

We need to be careful not to define the word 'industry' too narrowly. Its use nowadays embraces working environments from tourism to banking, from technology to entertainment. In this chapter, and for today's industrial mission, we should take the word to mean 'economic activity'. Nevertheless, we need to recognize that in the early days of industrial mission industrial chaplains seemed to concentrate much of their attention on large-scale 'metal bashing' in industrial cities.

During the two World Wars, chaplains served in the armed forces and other clergy worked in munitions factories. These padres were widely recognized as performing a very useful function and it therefore seemed a natural development, after the war and in the early 1950s, for 'padres' to visit factories to engage in counselling and evangelism. Initially these chaplains were engaged mostly in a personal ministry to individuals at work; however, Ted Wickham in 1940s and 1950s Sheffield soon adopted a different model for industrial mission. Wickham gathered together groups of people in the steel works and began to discuss with them the relevance of the Christian faith to such issues as industrial relationships and working practices. He was also concerned about the structure of the steel industry as an institution in Sheffield. Wickham's sector work was prophetic in nature rather than pastoral and evangelistic (though, of course, no easy distinction can be made between these).

In the 1950s, the Roman Catholic church in France, realizing that their priests were losing contact with the industrial working classes, sanctioned an experiment whereby priests obtained secular employment in factories. This 'worker priest' experiment was brought to an abrupt end when it was thought that the priests were becoming overpoliticised and were accused of being Communists. The French Protestant churches also began to establish sector ministries in industry, although their ministers did not visit factories on a regular basis. Nevertheless, there was an involvement in industrial issues and in the 1960s there was a series of reciprocal visits made between the French Protestant Industrial Mission and industrial missioners from the UK.

In Germany industrial mission was pioneered by Horst Szymanowski. To him, as to most involved in industrial mission at this time, the theology underpinning such mission was important. A young minister, when asked by Szymanowski what he was doing, replied that he was taking God into industry. To this Szymanowski retorted 'That will be an interesting experience for Almighty God. Where will you be taking him next, I wonder?'[2]

Foundations of industrial mission

In the UK, in addition to Ted Wickham, the first pioneers of industrial mission were Bill Wright in Teesdale, Ralph Stevens in Birmingham, Colin Cuttell in south London and Simon Phipps in Coventry. These people, together with Molly Batten, who ran the William Temple College in Rugby, and Cecilia Goodenough, theological consultant to the South London Industrial Mission, were the giants of their age. Their tenets for industrial mission were:

- God cannot be taken into industry – God is there already!
- The task is to discover the work of God and foster God's purposes.
- Industrial mission is Trinitarian: to care, to cross barriers, to engage in education and training (this corresponds to the Father who cares, the Son who reconciles and the Holy Spirit who leads us into truth).
- Pastoral care for individuals in industry is important, but it may be even more important to encourage industry to become a caring institution (it is no use setting up a first aid post in a factory if the machinery lacks proper guards!).
- Industrial chaplains are in a unique position to ask questions about a whole range of issues affecting well-being in the workplace.

From the earliest days of industrial mission, therefore, it has been recognized that chaplains are in a position to bring together a wide cross-section of people from industry into a safe environment to discuss matters which are contentious and potentially divisive. The church's ministry of reconciliation can, as in marriage counselling, be of great importance in economic life; but, like marriage itself, should not be undertaken (in the words of the Book of Common Prayer) 'unadvisedly, lightly or wantonly; but reverently, discreetly, soberly and in the fear of God'. I well remember saying to the Bishop of Birmingham, when he wanted to intervene in a strike at the British Leyland car plant in Longbridge, 'For God's sake, keep out of it'.

Industrial chaplains also soon became involved in education and training programmes in companies, alongside the various networks which bind companies together. In Croydon, the team worked alongside the Productivity Association and the Chamber of Commerce and organized a series of meetings and conferences on a wide range of issues including racial equality, the school-to-work transition, job satisfaction, industrial relationships and managing change. We established a quarterly magazine which was distributed in over fifty companies in the area. We also organized industrial harvest festivals, recruiting a choir from within industry and commerce for that purpose. At Christmas we attended a wide range of social events and often gave a special Christmas message during working hours. On these occasions the Bishop of Croydon would often be present to speak as well as to listen.

Staffing, payment and time commitment

It was not long after the earliest days of industrial mission that it was recognized that chaplaincy should be an ecumenical undertaking. It cannot be otherwise, as industry exists to bring together large numbers of people for one common purpose, namely to work. In the 1950s, 1960s and 1970s industrial relationships were poor and it would have been disastrous to add ecclesiastic divisions to the plethora of secular divisions which existed at the time. On the contrary, sector ministries, such as those in industry, are an important means by which Christian unity can be achieved. In 1968 the Industrial Mission Association (IMA) was formed to give a sense of identity to the movement. This ecumenical body provides support to chaplains, produces a monthly newsletter and holds a biannual conference. In a similar vein the Churches' Consortium on Industrial Mission was formed in 1975 to consider ecumenical and organizational aspects of the work. Meeting four times each year, it brought together representatives from all the major Christian denominations, as well as representatives from the Churches Together in Britain and Ireland, the Girls' Friendly Society and the IMA, and produced a series of 'policy' and 'recommended' papers describing good practice on various aspects of the work. In 1996, under the ecumenical 'Churches Together' the Consortium was superseded by the Churches' Co-ordinating Group for Mission in Industry and the Economy.

The question 'Who pays the chaplain?' arose at an early stage in industrial mission. Some felt that whilst it might be helpful for industry to make contributions to industrial mission funds (preferably held centrally by an ecumenical council), it was not helpful for chaplains to be paid directly by companies. The fear here was that 'He who pays the piper may want to call the tune'. Many industrial chaplains prefer to be neutral guests within their sector of economic activity. As such, they feel better able to raise questions without inhibitions. Even so, industrial chaplains have sometimes been asked to leave when questions they have raised have been seen as 'too near the mark'.

Some people ask why it is necessary to have full-time sector ministries in industry at all. 'Why', they ask, 'can this work not be done from a traditional congregational base?' Industrial mission can indeed be done this way. During my own ministry I have worked both as a full-time industrial chaplain, as vicar of a parish whilst also having a chaplaincy ministry and have worked in chaplaincy from a cathedral base. From this experience I would urge that industrial chaplains should, where possible, be freed from the task of maintaining church buildings and traditional congregations, in order to concentrate on 'front-line mission'.[3] This is especially true for those who lead a team of industrial chaplains, as the work can be very demanding if it is undertaken seriously. Chaplains who also have responsibility from a parochial church base, in charge of large buildings which are expensive to maintain, may be tempted to see their task in terms of a 'come to church' ministry.

Industrial chaplains work best in teams (for mutual support) and in these teams there should be a good mix of denominations as well as full and part-time chaplains. Chaplains have a twofold task: to 'interpret' the church to industry and to 'interpret' industry to the church, and this is better done with colleagues with whom to explore ideas and plan future ministry. Feedback to the church and especially to church leaders is essential. It is important that sector ministers do not work in isolation or become cut off from the mainstream church: teams can prevent this from happening.

The Sunday–Monday connection

'Bring them in, bring them in from the land of sin' may be a skit, but it does contain more than a grain of truth. Those in parochial ministry may be tempted to see lay people in congregations in terms of their ability to support the clergy rather than the other way round. Yet as sector ministers our principal task is to support and encourage lay people in their own front-line ministry and to send them out into the world to live and work there. I well remember the cry of anguish from a leader of a national organization who complained that, as a member of his local church, his vicar expected him to keep church accounts and clear birds' nests from the gutters. The vicar, however, seldom gave him the support he needed as a national leader in industry.

Pope John Paul II, in his encyclical *On Human Work* wrote that work is a fundamental dimension of human existence on earth. This being the case, a sector ministry alongside those engaged in the workplace is of fundamental importance. Human beings are created in the image of the creator God. All human work is therefore divine work, and this is as true of factory workers, those who work in supermarkets, bankers, airline pilots, as it is for doctors and priests. In this sense, all work is a vocation.

The basic task of industrial chaplains is to visit places of work to learn about economic activity and to exercise a ministry alongside those who work there. It might be asked 'How can this be done without holding up production?' It is not an easy matter and it is therefore essential that chaplains are trained in certain basic skills before they begin their work. Chaplains also need to be properly 'inducted' into each company they visit and to understand the context in which the particular industry is working. Without such training or understanding it is possible to create havoc! However, most of chaplains exercise their ministry with sensitivity and care, quietly moving around the workplace, often 'loitering with intent', raising questions, looking and listening. We try to speak to everyone (managers and workforce alike), we build up contacts, we are careful not to ram religion down people's throats. Whilst some areas in the company may be out of bounds (e.g. for safety or security reasons), we are not content with confining our ministry to canteen breaks, though these may present useful opportunities for extended conversations. Nor is it wise for chaplains to confine themselves to an office if they have one. People may find it physically or emotionally difficult to come to a chaplain's office. The chaplains should go to them! If chaplains encounter Christian fellowship groups already meeting in industry they support them but are careful not to become overidentified with them because chaplains should have a proper concern for everyone in their sector, not just Christians.

As a snapshot of the sorts of issues with which industrial chaplains engage, the team with which I was involved at Coventry will provide good examples. The facilities at Coventry cathedral were very good and the team was able to organize high-calibre conferences embracing a wide cross-section of people from 'both sides' of industry. Among subjects tackled were 'The quality of working life' (looking at job enrichment), 'Stress at work' and 'Industrial relationships'. In our conferences we always included a session on theological reflection when a serious attempt was made to relate the practical issues under discussion to relevant Christian insights. This process is known as 'Inductive theology'. Unlike Harold Wilson, who used the term 'theology' to describe anything which he regarded as irrelevant, industrial missioners regard theology as of vital importance to the whole of life. Theological themes such as creation, stewardship, human dignity, redemption, and many others, have much to say about the industrial context within which work is done.

There was an added international dimension at Coventry. The cathedral had developed a worldwide network of international contacts through its International Ministry. Coventry's industrial mission became part of that network. We had a close link with Berlin and regularly conveyed groups of managers, apprentices and trade union representatives to meet their counterparts in Berlin using our link with industrial mission in that city. Each visit would extend over a week or more and would include tours, visits to companies, meetings, theological reflection and an opportunity to visit East

Berlin, which in those days (with the Wall in place) was an exciting adventure. We were able to arrange reciprocal visits to the West Midlands for people from Berlin.

Whilst based in Coventry I had the privilege of a three-month visit to industrial mission in India where I was invited to be the visiting 'professor' at a training establishment in Durgapur. During the time there I was able to visit a number of industrial missions in various parts of the country and came to admire the dedication displayed by Indian sector ministers, who were very effective in empowering ordinary working people (especially those engaged in the motor industry and those who operated rickshaws). The increasingly worldwide dimension to industrial chaplaincy has also twice taken me to America, where on a three-month sabbatical I studied business ethics. The contacts made and knowledge gained there resulted in the foundation of two Centres for Business Ethics in the UK (in Birmingham and Sunderland).

Transforming institutions

Over the years industrial chaplaincy has increasingly shifted its emphasis from exclusively individual-based ministry to include issue-based ministry. An example of this is the work of the Churches' Industrial Group in Birmingham. Unemployment had begun to be a very serious problem in much of Britain during the 1980s and Birmingham's metal industry was devastated, losing over one-third of its metal manufacturing jobs. This job loss in the manufacturing sector also had an enormous knock-on effect in the service sector. The Churches' Industrial Group worked closely with the West Midlands Trade Union Congress in many ways, including organizing a number of marches and demonstrations to draw attention to the plight of those who were unemployed. Bishop Hugh Montefiore encouraged us to establish an 'Unemployment Commission' and we began to set up a number of practical projects. We obtained funding for these from the churches, the City Council and the government's Manpower Services Commission. Our first city-wide project, Inter-church Endeavour, consisted of a network of 'drop-in' centres all over Birmingham linked to a disused Victorian school which we acquired as a training centre. As well as practical skills, we encouraged unemployed people to be 'proactive'. We also established an Icebreaker Sales School to advise unemployed people how to construct job applications and prepare for interviews.

In 1986 we set up the Birmingham Churches' Managing Agency to administer projects on behalf of all the churches. Responding to changes in government policy we offered training in five core skills: clerical, computing, catering, construction and caring. The agency was managed by former unemployed people and in due course we encouraged a management 'buy-out'. The agency still flourishes and is a good example of what empowerment can achieve.

I have already mentioned one of the most recent projects, the Birmingham Centre for Business Ethics. The Centre has been established in conjunction with the Chamber of Commerce, the Institute of Management and the business schools of the three universities in Birmingham. Christians and non-Christians alike frequently find ethical issues at work difficult to reconcile. The Centre provides a forum for understanding that much of business cannot be seen as black and white, but as various shades of grey. Areas such as the late payment of commercial debt, ethical investment and environmental issues can all be examined and teased apart by experts and practitioners in industry. Compromise is sometimes regarded as a dirty word, but responsible compromise is often the only sensible procedure in working life. A former industrial chaplain, Bishop Simon Phipps, used the 'zig-zag' approach to illustrate this. It is not always easy to head straight for the desired goal (what he called 'Kingdom values'). Sometimes we are in the zig and sometimes we are in the zag, but we still press towards the goal.[4] This is what incarnation means in practice.

Conclusion

There is much more that could be said about industrial mission. The nature of work is constantly evolving due to technological change, and industry is not just locally based but, through the nature of our human interrelatedness, is now global in dimension. The nature of employment is changing too; one person in one job for life is a thing of the past and today there is much talk of 'downsizing' and far less job security. All these dimensions impact upon the quality of life for everyone, whether in employment or not, and it is vital that the church is fully involved in this as in every other sphere of life. I pray that the church may never forget the fundamental importance of sector ministry in industry. The gap between the church and industry needs to be continually bridged. Our task remains to further the Kingdom of God there. The Kingdom is not confined to the church, nor is it confined to industry: the Kingdom comes wherever God's will is discerned and fostered.

Notes

1 E. R. Wickham, *Church and People in an Industrial City* (London: Lutterworth Press, 1957).
2 See Horst Szymanowski, *The Christian Witness in an Industrial Society* (London: Collins, 1966).
3 For further discussion of this and other issues for industrial chaplaincy see Denis

Claringbull, *Front Line Mission: Ministry in the Market Place* (Norwich: Canterbury Press, 1994).

4   This idea is explored in Simon Phipps, *God on Monday* (London: Hodder and Stoughton, 1966).

10

Police

Barry Wright

The development of police chaplaincy

Police chaplaincy, as a sector of ministry within the mission of the church, has expanded very significantly throughout the United Kingdom (and indeed the world) over the last few years. There are three hundred chaplains from all the major Christian denominations in the UK. In the USA most states employ full-time police chaplains, and some mainland European countries (e.g. Germany and France) also employ police chaplains. In the UK most police chaplains are part-time appointees. They may be charged with the pastoral oversight of one particular police station, or perhaps a larger unit such as a police division or in some cases one chaplain may have responsibility for an entire Force. There are six full-time appointments – to the Metropolitan Police, the Greater Manchester Police, the West Midlands Police, Durham Constabulary, Hampshire Constabulary and West Mercia Constabulary.

The present-day chaplains to the police service are exercising a ministry which is as old as the police service itself, albeit in a radically different environment. Before the 1960s most police forces were small borough constabularies with strengths of not more than a hundred officers. The local village or town 'bobby' lived in a police house in the centre of the community he policed, and was as much a part of the local establishment, as was the vicar or doctor. Similarly, the position of the senior police officer placed its holder amongst the eminent citizens of the area and in consequence the relationship between police and clergy was based on familiarity, shared concerns and personal contact.

The 1960s saw the amalgamation of police forces into County and Metropolitan areas; police houses were sold off, and it became rare for an officer serving a particular community to have any involvement with it beyond his or her commitment to the policing profession. As a consequence, the pastoral relationship between officers and community grew more distant. The same period also brought about a significant shift in attitude towards the police. Traffic offences, political protest and soft drug taking brought people into direct confrontation and conflict with the police on a scale never experienced before. This led to feelings of widespread disenchantment with and suspicion of the police role in society and its methods. Such feelings were fuelled by the revelation of a number of police corruption and malpractice scandals during the same period. The amalgam of changing attitudes and the loss of the organic relationship between the church and police opened up a significant breach in relations between the two institutions. A number of police officers and church people sought to heal the divide (most notably Archdeacon Len Tyler, when he was Principal of William Temple College), but by the early 1980s the breach seemed as wide as ever.[1] In 1984 the Board of Social Responsibility of the Church of England published a report voicing considerable concerns about the attitudes, ethos and practices of the Metropolitan Police.[2] At this time police officers were particularly sensitive to what they regarded as unfair and hostile criticism, and there was a feeling that no effort had been made to meet with the police or to understand their situation with its host of problems.

Since that time, however, both the church and the police have made considerable efforts to gain an appreciation of each other's problems. In part these efforts were inspired by the Archbishops' Commission on Urban Priority Areas which produced the report *Faith in the City*,[3] which encouraged the appointment of police chaplains; the call of successive Metropolitan Police Commissioners and Chief Constables to adopt a 'multi-agency approach' in tackling police/community issues; and by the active participation of clergy and church members on Police Consultative Groups which were set up as a result of the Scarman enquiry.[4]

One consequence of the re-established dialogue between the church and the police has been the appointment of police chaplains by the majority of police forces in the United Kingdom. A need was perceived to extend independent pastoral care for police officers and civilian employees of the police service, given the increasingly complex and demanding nature of their work. This has led to what one might call the 'reinvention' of ministry to the police.

Current models of police chaplaincy in the United Kingdom

In 1996 the Revd Richard Armitage, an Anglican priest, voluntary chaplain to the police in the Vale of Evesham and convening chaplain for the West Mercia Constabulary, was granted a Home Office Police Research Award to study the concept and present state of police chaplaincy. He discovered that 30 of the 39 English constabularies have a recognized system of chaplaincy. In addition to these constabulary appointments there has also been a full-time chaplain appointed at the Police Staff College, Bramshill, Hampshire. Chaplaincy also formally exists in one of the four Welsh constabularies. In another Welsh constabulary, a serving police officer, who is a non-stipendiary minister, works closely with the welfare department and responds to requests for support as they are referred to him. There are chaplains in one of the eight Scottish constabularies and chaplains in both Guernsey and Jersey. There is no official chaplain in the Isle of Man, but the Anglican bishop of that diocese has been designated by the constabulary as the person who may be approached should the need arise. In the Royal Ulster Constabulary there is no chaplaincy, although a number of ministers have been identified by their churches to fulfil the role of chaplain should this be considered helpful by police commanders.

Armitage's research found that the chaplains' work situations are diverse and include the following:

*   Single nominated voluntary chaplains, whose primary duty is to fulfil ceremonial duties and pastoral roles. Here the pastoral role may be limited by the availability of time.
*   Single chaplains working in conjunction with some other ecclesiastical responsibility.
*   Individual chaplains working in isolation from each other in geographical pockets, which may or may not be co-ordinated.
*   Part-time chaplains working to a structured geographical area across a constabulary.
*   Full-time chaplains working with a team of part-time voluntary chaplains.
*   Full-time chaplains working without the support of part-time voluntary chaplains.

An analysis of all chaplaincy posts indicates that 70 per cent of the voluntary chaplains are ordained members of the Church of England, whilst the remaining 30 per cent of the chaplains belong to other Christian denominations including Baptist, Methodist, Pentecostal, Roman Catholic, Church of Scotland, Salvation Army, United Reformed Church, Church in Wales and the Evangelical Church. There is also one Rabbi acting as a chaplain.

The selection and method of appointment of chaplains varies widely. Full-time chaplains are normally appointed by the diocesan bishop in consultation with the chief officer of police, each chaplain having a clearly defined contract of employment and job description. For the appointment of voluntary chaplains, however, there is no standard procedure in place. In some instances consultation over the appointment of a chaplain has been at the instigation of the church, whether through the interest of a member of the local clergy in the course of his ministry or as a deliberate initiative on the part of a diocese or ecumenical body.

Qualities required in a police chaplain

The basis of an effective chaplaincy is the trust and confidence that the police service has in the individual chaplain or chaplains that minister within it. They must have empathy with, and an understanding of, the police service and the pressures faced by police officers in today's society. The Home Office paper details the results of a questionnaire given to police personnel on the qualities of a chaplain.[5] The response to the characteristics these personnel believed to be essential can be grouped into the categories of:

- listening skills
- human sensitivity
- personal knowledge
- availability
- confidentiality
- diplomacy and discretion
- common sense
- realism and pragmatism
- objectivity
- experience of working with people
- a non-judgmental and unpatronizing attitude.

As well as looking at professional skills, police officers also asked that chaplains should possess certain human virtues and strengths including:

- understanding
- empathy/sympathy
- compassion
- patience
- a sense of humour
- approachability
- caring attitude
- sincerity
- calmness
- friendliness
- sociability.

It is clear from these responses that police personnel expect to find in a chaplain a definite strength of personality and character including honesty, integrity and impartiality. It is interesting to note that only a few respondents specified that a chaplain should demonstrate a depth of faith and spirituality. Other qualities which were also mentioned were openness and broadness of mind, credibility, maturity and wisdom.

The role of the police chaplain

The terms of reference for police chaplains are tightly drawn. Chaplains are 'guests' of the police, they are not police employees, their role and function places them outside the police command structure. Chaplains are privileged to minister to members of an organization which has considerable and urgent demands placed upon it, and which is privy to very sensitive information. In this independent role a chaplain is available to all ranks and grades of the police service from the chief officer of police to the newest recruit – regardless of the officer's religious commitment, or lack of it. In this environment, the chaplain has to exercise great care in gaining the trust of officers and civilian support staff. A willingness to meet with officers and be alongside them in all aspects of their duties – to be an independent, confidential 'listening ear' – is the crucial role of the police chaplain. Accompanying a night patrol, attending the scene of major disasters or fatal road traffic accidents, helping in the delivery of a death message, conducting the funeral of a deceased police officer, are all regular aspects of some chaplains' ministries.

However, in the course of all things that a chaplain does, a critical distance needs to be maintained – the police service has generated a very powerful and embracing organizational structure, and there are strong temptations to adapt to this unquestioningly. Lord Runcie, formerly Archbishop of Canterbury, coined the term 'critical solidarity' with reference to the church's involvement with the police. The phrase serves well to describe the particular stance necessary for the chaplain's role. Some feel that the political and personal sensitivity of the role of police chaplaincy does, to some extent, set it apart from other forms of sector ministry, such as industrial or hospital chaplaincy, but this may only be a matter of degree.

Police chaplaincy and other sector ministries

I should like to suggest that police chaplaincy may share four central aspects with other types of chaplaincy.

Sacramental
The role of the police officer in today's society is extremely diverse. Officers are required to perform a multitude of different functions, some of which may

turn out to be complex, even contradictory. Simultaneously, a police officer may be called upon to be a crime fighter and a crime preventer, a crowd controller, an intelligence officer, a social worker, a manager of resources and many other things besides.

The police service *Statement of Common Purpose and Values* states that 'the purpose of the police is to uphold to law fairly and firmly; prevent crime, pursue and bring to justice those who break the law; keep the Queen's peace; protect, help and reassure the community they serve'. In practice, this means that the police have a series of roles that cluster round the notion of attempting to minimize disruption to law-abiding citizens, and doing all in their power to ensure that people can live in safety – the majority of any individual police officer's time is spent in this protecting, reassuring and helping function.

In many respects, policing is a balancing act and has a delicate and exposed role in trying to maintain some form of tranquillity, without undermining the legitimate interests a country's citizens. The many facets of the police role appear to some to be a paradox and police officers often feel under attack and misunderstood. In his paper, Armitage makes the point that the Christian priest and pastor fully understands the concept of this crucifixion of misunderstanding. The priest sacramentally bears the cross of Christ and can identify with those officers who are misunderstood by their communities and suffer as a consequence.

The police chaplain is one who seeks to serve, service and encourage. She signifies the presence of the incarnational God with police officers in their work of maintaining order and law and with the police service as an organization in society.

Pastoral

A major part of the police chaplain's work is to minister to police officers in their work situation and meet with them at their point of need. This is about 'good shepherding' – being there for Christ's sake – recognizing their voice – knowing and being known – and 'going the extra mile'. A police chaplain cannot be expected to have had all the experience that a serving police officer would have had, but the chaplain works with the whole person in seeking to listen, support, comfort and counsel without a hidden agenda. It is by 'being around' and 'loitering with intent' that a chaplain will get to know the organization and individuals and break down barriers, regardless of rank, and build up trust. In this 'listening role' a chaplain will identify issues and problems that are a cause for concern, and in turn can offer empathy, support, advice and guidance, and if necessary refer on for appropriate professional help. More and more police officers are involved in traumatic incidents in the normal course of their duties, and the chaplain seeks, alongside colleagues in police occupational health staff and welfare counsellors, to assure all personnel that they are normal people responding in normal ways to abnormal situations and events.

The chaplain, along with other ministers of religion, has a significant role to play when police personnel are faced with loss or bereavement and is able to assist them in talking about and expressing their grief and to pray with and for them, if they so desire.

Prophetic

When chaplains have become sufficiently established in their posts they can gain trust, confidence and credibility within the police organization. With this trustworthiness in place, they are able to raise the difficult questions about the work and the role of the police as servants to the public. Theirs is a voice which is sufficiently imbued with the culture of policing and may be listened to; others outside the force may not be listened to in the same way. Chaplains are also able to address, to challenge and to clarify the moral and ethical questions faced both by the police and the church.

Bridge-builder

The priest or minister, by virtue of the vows made at ordination, acts as a bridge-builder between God and humankind. It is part of the police chaplain's priestly vocation to act as a link between the police and the church, and through knowledge of the police structure and ethos to speak authoritatively to the church on matters concerning the police.

Dr George Carey, Archbishop of Canterbury, in an address to police recruits in 1995, emphasized that the partnership in service between the police and the church at the hard, ugly end of human life is to be valued and nurtured. He went on to say that both the police and the church, in their different spheres, attempt to do their work in the face of increased criticism and scepticism. Both police and clergy are left to pick up the pieces caused by wider social failure – and are often blamed for them. This may be usefully remembered when, from time to time, police and clergy find themselves working together, picking up society's failings and having to handle the sad and nasty parts of human existence which other people may turn their back on. This is a partnership which the Archbishop would like to see strengthened, as both organizations have a shared interest in community values.

It is as part of this bridge-building role that the chaplain is able to foster close working relationships between local clergy and the police. There is often misunderstanding of the respective roles, especially among clergy and police officers who are new to their work, and the chaplain can be the 'resource person' to arrange placements and seminars to engender good working practices. Police chaplaincy can build those bridges and facilitate the mutual learning of both the church and the police.

Conclusion

The expansion of chaplaincy to the police over the ten years from the late 1980s has been valuable in the help and support it provides to a sector of our society which is coming under increasing pressure and scrutiny.

The presence of a chaplain within the police environment is a sign of God's continual presence in every sphere of human activity, but especially where there are difficult choices to be made and relations between human beings are most strained. The police service has been given the task of having to deal in an area of human activity where human sin and selfishness make themselves most evident. Police officers often operate where the normal interactions between human beings break down; they are society's ministers of human failure. The Christian faith is fundamentally concerned with brokeness and failure, and with the hurt and damage which such failure visits upon all whom it affects.

The presence of a chaplain to the police is, in some way, a sign of God's encouragement for and a validation of the work of the police service in trying to contain and constrain such damaging failure within our society. Through sensitive working, police chaplains can play a significant part in seeking to heal and build up those within the police service who constantly have to deal with the damaging effects of our human failure. Through prayer, support and encouragement, police chaplains can see their ministry as part of God's sustaining and nurturing activity in a fallen world.

Notes

1   For an examination of this see Len Tyler, *Police and Community* (London: Church Information Office, 1969).
2   *Policing in a Democratic Society* (London: Church House Publishing, 1984).
3   *Faith in the City: Archbishop of Canterbury's Report on Urban Priority Areas* (London: Church House Publishing, 1985).
4   Lord Scarman's *Report on the Causes of the Brixton Disorders* had been published four years earlier.
5   Richard Armitage, *Police Chaplaincy – Servant to the Service* (London: Home Office, 1996).

11

Prisons

Harry Potter

A brief history of imprisonment

The 1991 riot in HMP Strangeways began in the chapel. Where else? It was the only prison building big enough for a mob to congregate. The great Victorian prisons, of which Strangeways is but one, were designed to isolate evil behind impenetrable walls where God and the Devil would wrestle for the soul of every felon. Christianity was at the heart of imprisonment and the focal point of each prison was the chapel.

Before the nineteenth century prisons were few in number and were ramshackle affairs used for debtors or for felons awaiting trial or execution. You were either whipped or pilloried for minor offences or transported or hanged for major ones. Towards the end of the eighteenth century two divergent influences converged to bring about a transformation in penal thinking. Utilitarians considered that the purpose of punishment was not to avenge crime but to prevent it, and that the way in which it was administered should reflect the social good and the offender's needs. Criminals were merely sick, not wicked. In so far as they were rational beings they could be deterred by severe punishments; in so far as they were defective machines they could be repaired by social engineering. This dual purpose could best be served by a prison system designed to mould and change character as well as to deter offenders. Christians, on the other hand, were appalled by the state of ordinary gaols and attracted to the possibility of inducing repentance in felons rather than merely punishing their behaviour. Nonconformists in particular, stressing the identification of all persons in sin, believed that criminals were not intrinsically different from the rest of society. They too could be redeemed. As a result of these twin pressures, Parliament passed the Penitentiary Act of 1779 which attempted to combine the monastic or Quaker ideals of silence and solitude being a stimulant to reflection, repentance and regeneration, the utilitarian desire for social control and scientific observation, and the desire of both for deterrence. Red-brick schools and colleges sprang up to educate and train the upper and middle classes in muscular Christianity and in their God-given duty to rule. Gothic revival churches, with their ranks of dark hard pews, were consecrated to ensure Christian conformity among the urban poor. Lunatics were controlled and isolated in asylums, workers employed – or enslaved – in factories. It was in keeping with these that the great penitentiaries – 'virtue factories' – were built to isolate, employ and re-create the criminal. In Pentonville, built in 1842, men lived for up to three years in total silence and solitude, wearing masks and sitting in individual cubicles when in chapel so that their undistracted attention would be on the chaplain admonishing them to change their ways. Reformation of the soul was equated with breaking of the spirit. In prolonged solitary confinement the prisoner was left to his own remorse and became his own tormentor. Many went mad. It was a distortion of what the Christian reformers had sought. The penitentiary system withered as opposition to it grew and its ineffectiveness became manifest, leaving the grim prisons still standing and those prisons still full. Disillusion with the reformatory ideal set in and the system turned half circle, as it has several times since. The regime became brutally penal: harsh sentences, harsh conditions, harsh treatment. The ethos was to discipline and punish.[1]

Christian reforming zeal, however, was not to be silenced. Prisoners could not be coerced nor remodelled but they could be educated and trained. Towards the end of the nineteenth century liberal opinion, spurred on by the poignant and revelatory letters of Oscar Wilde, seemed to triumph, culminating in the Gladstone Report of 1895 which described prisons as places of 'treatment and reform'. The first prison rule states the aim of imprisonment in the following terms: 'the training and treatment of convicted prisoners shall be to encourage and assist them to live a good and useful life'. The 1988 'Statement of Purpose' encapsulates the dual role of 'look[ing] after prisoners with humanity' and helping 'them to lead useful lives in custody and after release'. Whatever the government or the public mood, this emphasis still survives, sometimes wilting, sometimes reviving, but showing persistence and tenacity. It is persistently under threat from gross overcrowding, longer and longer sentences for more and more people, overworked staff, decaying buildings and an emphasis on security which precludes many erstwhile initiatives.

Throughout this progression or regression or revolution in penal thought and practice, chaplains have been an integral and indelible part of the prison system, at different times ministering to the condemned, organizing welfare and education, administering the sacraments, praying for their charges. To this day all prisons have a chapel, all prisons have a chaplain, all prisoners have a right to practise their faith.

The role of the chaplain

A former Chaplain General defined the role in the following terms:

> The Chaplain is there to be used, to recognize the individual as an individual, something more than a number, a prisoner, a problem, a threat, or even a client. He is there to love the unlikeable, to protect whatever rights he has, going to where people are, accepting them as they are, encouraging as much response as they are capable of making. He will need sympathy, resilience and patience. He is there to listen more than to talk. He is there to contribute friendship, significance, hope, purpose and forgiveness to those who have been deprived of these attributes or have lost all appreciation of them.

It may only be to call *persons* by their *Christian* names, rather than prisoners by their number. It may be to touch prisoners when they cry. It may be to show compassion rather than revulsion. It may be to phone a partner to tell her that John is all right. It may be to allow yourself to be made use of and not mind. It may be to take up individual cases which are costly in terms of time, money and reputation. It may be to tackle injustice, institutional and individual. It may be to work to change the way prisons are, and the way society perceives prisoners, and to reform a society which at least in part abets in the criminalization and degradation of a section of the community.

Chaplains have an inbuilt prejudice in their favour. They are not governors, 'screws', or 'shrinks'. They are trusted until they abuse that trust. Being so closely interwoven in the fabric of such an institution provides chaplains with a unique opportunity to speak to the unchurched and minister to immediate and often raw need.

To portray the life of a contemporary chaplain is to paint a self-portrait. My association with prisons and criminals spans many years, from visiting Borstals in student days to visiting imprisoned parishioners when curate of St Paul's, Deptford. When I was appointed a college chaplain, I was invited to assist, during the holidays, at Wormwood Scrubs. After three years of substitution work, in 1987 I became the full-time deputy chaplain.

The Wormwood Scrubs experience

The Scrubs is a microcosm of prison life, having two wings for remand prisoners awaiting trial, one wing for those serving under 18 months, and one for life-sentence prisoners. The morning duties included visiting all the newly arrived remands, those in the hospital or in isolation – either for their own protection on Rule 43 ('nonces' and 'grasses') or as punishment in the 'Seg' – and responding to applications. Sometimes an inmate wanted a Bible or prayer card, sometimes a prayer or a library book or a phone call home, or just a chat. It was sticking-plaster work, but valuable for all that. By contrast, the afternoons would be taken up in visiting the lifer wing. Life-sentence prisoners are invariably the pleasantest and easiest to get on with. They have time to think and take stock, they know where they will be for years to come, they have incentives to change and mature. They are often deeply remorseful. It was very relaxing after a hard morning responding to the instant needs and anxieties of the remands to unwind over a cup of tea in a cell with three or four murderers.

The chapel, a Portland stone listed basilica the size of small cathedral, lies at the very centre of the Scrubs. Paintings of the apostles ring the apse, the models for whom were prisoners when the chapel was built. The altar frontal was woven and given by Queen Mary, the piano given by Ivor Novello, who had been imprisoned during the Second World War for black marketeering.

This was the splendid setting for weekday services and Sunday High Mass, the latter complete with inmate servers and incense. Services in the Scrubs were not as services elsewhere. There was a frisson of excitement and element of unpredictability absent outside. Impromptu lay participation in the liturgy was often in evidence. One Sunday a local Bishop had been rudely received, and during Communion eggs had been thrown at the 'nonces'. The following week, as preacher, I admonished the congregation. Not a murmur, not an egg. A few days later a much tattooed young man on A wing asked to see me. He had been one of the ringleaders and had not slept for three nights after my sermon. He was so ashamed of what he had done. Warming to his appreciation of my preaching, I drew out his story. He had another sin to confess. He had once attended church. After the collection had been taken he felt compelled to make his way into the vestry and steal the money. I told him what he must do: confess to the priest and offer to make up for it by voluntary work. This he had already done, he told me: the priest had 'shopped' him to the police, and so now he was serving 18 months. One Confirmation service was highly charged as a young lifer – and confirmand – read St Paul's strictures on murderers not inheriting the Kingdom of God.

So much of the gospel was illuminated within the shadows of the Scrubs. Our 'theological' concepts – guilt, repentance, forgiveness, oppression, good and evil, justice and injustice, humanity and dignity – are common currency in a prison context. Biblical stories of violence, cupidity and self-sacrifice were lived out on the wings and each prisoner told his own story of the prodigal son or his own 'prison' version of the Good Samaritan. God seemed hell-bent on choosing the dodgy, the deviant or the outlaw as the instruments of his purpose. Cain, the first murderer, was not executed but given a life sentence, forever bearing the mark of conviction and protection, a fratricide who was the founder of urban civilization. Jacob was a conman, conning his own father and brother. Moses was a terrorist prepared to murder to engineer a prison break. David instigated a contract killing of a faithful servant to cover up his own adultery. The Jews, God's chosen people, were prisoners first in Egypt, then in Babylon. Jeremiah, the prophet, was a political prisoner left to die in solitary confinement. John the Baptist was imprisoned and executed in prison. At the beginning of his ministry, Jesus announced that he had come to set the prisoner free. Three years later, wanted by the police as a subversive, he was betrayed by one of his disciples, the 'supergrass' Judas. Taken before a kangaroo court, arraigned on trumped-up charges before false witnesses and condemned to death, Jesus was another victim of a gross miscarriage of justice and the irreversible finality of capital punishment. He was judicially murdered: 'grassed up, stitched up, strung up', not in a cathedral between two candles but on a cross between two thieves. In his death agony, deserted by his friends, rejected by his people and abandoned by his father, he could still forgive those who crucified him and speak words of comfort to the thief who asked for it, reassuring him that the first Christian in heaven would be a common criminal, like himself.

Christian ethics provides an equally challenging perspective behind bars. 'All have sinned and fallen short of the glory of God' – prisoner and prison officer, criminal and chaplain. It is not the righteous sitting in judgement over the wicked, not the good against the bad, but the respectable exercising power over the disreputable; and that is very different. Who is worse: the burglar who steals your video or the adulterer who steals your happiness, and wrecks your security? The former goes to Crown Court, the latter only to the divorce court. Love your enemies! Does that include the 'nonce' on Rule 43, the 'grass' in the seg, the 'screw' who knocked back your parole?

Chaplains must be wary of counterfeit. Faith can often be seen as a panacea when it is no more than a placebo. Vulnerable prisoners may want a religion which seems to solve all their problems, and may eagerly embrace a simplistic, all-encompassing but unsearching salvationism. There is a real danger, not so much that shallow-rooted faith will wilt, but that it will camouflage. The rapist who believes that with his new-found faith all his problems have gone is a very dangerous man. He is not painfully and thoroughly cleaning the wound but merely plastering over the pus. All may have sinned but some sins are worse than others. It is disturbing when someone who is in for pretty nasty robberies says that in the eyes of God all sins are equally hateful. Gandhi cannot be equated with Hitler and someone who cannot distinguish between the two is morally inadequate.

Working with young offenders

After the Scrubs, I was posted to Aylesbury Young Offenders Institution. This is the only maximum security facility for under 21-year-olds, and the only one holding Category A prisoners, the most secure prison categorization. When I arrived, Aylesbury held 300 long-term and life sentence young offenders, ten of whom were Category A. When I left four years later numbers had dropped by a third. These were good times to be in the service. The wheel was turning in a progressive direction. The 1991 Criminal Justice Act would reduce numbers further; the Woolf Report would improve conditions.[2]

As usually the only full-time chaplain, the Anglican inevitably heads the chaplaincy team. As such I had to administer the chaplaincy, organize services, sit on a variety of prison boards – suicide prevention, home leave, race relations – address a large number of public meetings. In the wider arena I was asked to assist with *New Life*, the Prison Service Chaplaincy Review, and to contribute articles on penal policy to other journals. To marry my insider's experience with their outsiders' perspective I joined the Howard League and the Prison Reform Trust.

The Methodist minister, Catholic nun and I got on together and got on with the work together. If the nun visited the block she visited everyone there, not just the Catholics. Some services, especially Ash Wednesday and the Carol Service, were shared. Ordinands from Cuddesdon and St Stephen's House theological colleges – wearing dog-collars – did placements and were encouraged to act as chaplains. A Pentecostal choir came in once a month to take the main morning service. Seventh-day Adventists and other Evangelical churches came in to run groups and occasionally lead worship. I encouraged the Buddhist minister to give meditation classes in chapel and most of the participants were chapel regulars. The Sikh minister visited regularly. For many months we could not get a Muslim minister and on Fridays I became the honorary Imam and ran groups with the Muslim prisoners. The first Rastafarian visiting minister was appointed, chaperoned by an Ethiopian Orthodox Archimandrite.

Chapel was always well attended and challenging. Order had to be maintained. A few inmates were periodically banned, an action that merely seemed to make chapel the 'in' place to be. Congregational participation was frequent and novel. Being challenged on points in a sermon was a common-place and some in the congregation would remember that you had said something different the year before. The chapel was also a place to relax over tea or coffee, biscuits and cigarettes. Sunday afternoons saw another exclusive society – Culture Club – for those interested in watching 'improving films' and operas. Few realized they had this interest before they joined but attitudes soon changed, and applications for membership always outstripped places.

Chaplains are usually responsible for appointing and regulating prison visitors, and at Aylesbury we built up one of the largest schemes in the country. Volunteers from the community, after vetting and a little training, were asked to visit prisoners who requested their services. The demand always outstretched the resource. Not all were Christian, but most were. Some also attended chapel regularly, bringing flowers and biscuits with them.

Working closely with other disciplines was the key to success. Statutory duties could be performed in a few minutes each day. There was rarely anyone in the hospital and the segregation block was usually no more than a quarter full. As chaplain I had more time to analyse problems and suggest solutions than anyone else, and when I tried to initiate improvements I always included prison and probation officers, psychologists, and the psychiatrist. For over a year I had visited the Category A prisoners because they were locked up for 23 hours a day and denied access to education, recreation and work. No one knew why. A committee was set up, and recommendations were made and largely accepted. As a result, the regime for Category As was vastly improved, and I could visit them less often. Lifer family days were another initiative that came from the chaplaincy but involved all other disciplines. The parents, siblings or partners of prisoners were invited into the prison for a whole day. They visited the cells and wings, met the officers who looked after their boy, had lunch and were provided with a lot of information as to how the lifer system operated. These days were an enormous success. Mums broke down in tears of relief having at last seen where their sons dwelt and that the officers on their wings were human after all. The reality of prison was not as bad as the image that the families had. Knowing that officers could now contact their parents if they misbehaved, inmate behaviour improved. The officers welcomed the opportunity to show their humanity and do something more constructive than merely locking people up.[3]

Along with my colleagues in the other disciplines I was asked to write regular reports on the lifers and attend their review boards. These had to be taken very seriously. Lives are literally in your hands. The chaplain has a unique opportunity to get to know his charges. He alone among the professionals in a prison has a cell key, he often is the only member of staff trusted with confidences, confidences it is assumed he will not break. He may be able to form a fuller and rounder picture of the particular prisoner than anyone else. His opinions, and the quality of his advocacy for his parishioner, may profoundly affect that parishioner's progress through the prison system and even the length of time which he serves.

The call of the wild

The role of the prison chaplain within the modern prison system does not depend on status or statute. The Conservative government of the 1980s and 1990s attempted both to undermine the Prison Officers' Union and impose new structures and working patterns on the prison service. The chaplaincy was put in the Inmate Activities Group, under a junior governor. Many felt that Christianity – or perhaps their own position – was being diminished within the prison system. Fears were largely unfounded. Perhaps I was fortunate in working in two fairly progressive prisons – the Scrubs and Aylesbury – but I always found that those with something to contribute had influence. It was not your status but your contribution that counted. Too often chaplains have been of poor calibre, unable and unwilling to take a larger role in the prison system, yet craving status and recognition. When the House of Lords reported on life-sentence prisoners there were contributions from the Buddhist Chaplaincy Service and the Quakers but none from the mainstream Christian denominations. Time and again the Prison Service Chaplaincy has not contributed to issues of prison reform, parole, privatization or the Woolf Report. If you have something to contribute, good well-thought ideas, and have established a basis of trust with the authorities, change for the better is quite possible. Where chaplains fail is when they are perceived to be visionless, cynical, 'screws with dog-collars' by the prisoners, or undisciplined anachronisms – 'sky-pilots' – by the officers. A cell left unlocked after a visit, a refusal to inform officers when you are on the wing, a bit of prison gossip being spread, and a chaplain is distrusted, disliked or dismissed as irrelevant.

Prison service chaplaincy needs applicants who are intellectually and socially robust enough to work in the noisy, chaotic and disruptive atmosphere of a prison; spiritual enough to survive without the normal structures of support, versatile enough to be trusted by prisoners and prison officers, thoughtful enough to make constructive and radical criticisms of an institution which feeds them, mature enough to know when they have stayed in it long enough. The hours are short, the pay good, the work exciting, the rewards considerable, the experience and opportunities unique.

Notes

1   On this whole development see Michael Ignatief, *A Just Measure of Pain* (London: Macmillan, 1978).

2 These conditions were dashed by Home Secretary Michael Howard's futile but draconian measures.
3 A full account of this initiative entitled 'Teabags for the Chaplain' can be found on pp. 63–73 in vol. 9 (1992), of *New Life*, the Prison Service Chaplaincy Review.

12

Retail trade

Lyn Jamieson

High five to a colleague as we meet on the mall. 'Yo Lyn! What did ye think aboot the game?' We are in Geordieland at Europe's largest shopping and leisure complex, the MetroCentre, and it is the day after one of Newcastle United's games. We are ecstatic that the Toon Army have won! This is a typical encounter in my ministry as a retail chaplain; it is a real privilege sharing in people's lives, with all the joys and sorrows these bring.

There has been a full-time chaplain in post since the centre opened. The concept of 'out-of-town' shopping in this country was pioneered by Sir John Hall and the MetroCentre led the way for other similar centres. Sir John had visited shopping malls in North America and felt that this was the way shopping could go in the United Kingdom. Collaboration between Sir John, the Church Commissioners, the Northumbrian Industrial Mission Team and the Centre's Management confirmed the appointment of the Centre's first chaplain, the Revd John Hammersley, in 1986. The job of a retail chaplain was virtually unknown then and the time was one of enterprise and adventure. In this sector, the wheel still had to be invented. John Hammersley firmly established retail chaplaincy as a distinctive chaplaincy within industrial mission. Never before had the concept been known on such a scale. The Church Commissioners agreed to pay the stipend and to fund the post for ten years. Today it is jointly funded by the Church Commissioners and Capital Shopping Centres (MetroCentre's owners). John stayed for seven years and it was due to these partnerships and creativity that the first full-time post of retail chaplain prospered.

Availability or not?

Every unit in the centre is given a card from me to display on their staff notice board. It has a picture of me smiling at them (who wants a miserable face?) and it tells them 'I am here to be alongside those who work at the MetroCentre. I am often available if anyone needs help or a quiet word.' The card also tells staff where they can find or contact me. When I showed the card to one of the centre's workers she said 'Why aren't you *always* available?' Tongue in cheek I answered that the charter for the work I do was stating the truth and that I couldn't be available all the time! The product I deliver – my time, care and thought – is not *ceaselessly* available and I feel that I should not give the impression that it is. But I am *often* available, either by the regular visits which I make to the units, at the meetings that I attend, in my office by telephone or in person, or simply meeting people on the malls as I wander around. It is amazing the number of people I do meet within the centre and some of the most profound conversations can happen whilst idly leaning over the railings of the first floor. Although looking relaxed and nonchalant, deep thoughts and involved ideas are talked through, maybe for a few minutes, maybe for half an hour. Chaplains are some of the few people with time available to give to others, therefore, as I am walking through the malls, I try and be approachable by walking slowly so that I can be accosted (in the nicest possible way). As well as this ministry to shops staff and shoppers, I am available to those who work 'behind the scenes'. These are the control room staff, the gardeners, those in technical services, the people on the Customer Services desk and the management and marketing staff. I am there for the security and cleaning teams. A lot of these people I count as my friends and many are wonderfully supportive of the job I do.

Sunday trading

These two dreaded words constitute one of the most talked about topics in my job. Sunday trading in England legally began in August 1994, just seven weeks after I took up my post. The Sunday Trading Bill went through Parliament at the time I was interviewed for the chaplain's job. As I expected, I was asked for my opinion on the subject, and explained that I felt that shops could not really be made to stay closed if the law says they may open. At the time the Church Commissioners owned the MetroCentre and were themselves thinking through the issues involved in Sunday trading. The Commissioners already had experience of Sunday trading in Scotland, as they partly owned the St Enoch Centre in the centre of Glasgow. MetroCentre opened legally for trading on Sunday 28 August 1994.

I am not in agreement with Sunday trading, although not because it might keep people away from church. Statistics over the last few years have indicated that declining church attendance is not entirely due to Sunday trading; a few people may have to work on Sunday and miss church, but they are in the minority. Trading on Sunday means that society does not now have a communal day of rest, pause, recreation and refreshment. Mike Starkey in *Born to Shop* documents well the pros and cons of Sunday trading.[1] He writes that Winston Churchill believed Sunday should be special. In *The Daily Telegraph* of 27 December 1933 Churchill said: 'Sunday is the necessary pause in the national life activity; it is essentially the day of emancipation from the compulsion and strain of daily work; it is the birthright of every British subject, a day of personal and spiritual opportunities.' I and many others feel that way in 1998, although Sunday is now a day like any other. There is a hustle and bustle. We are fast losing the opportunity to relax together, to pause collectively for thought, to share a day for refreshment. The ethos of Sunday cannot be found on any other day.

It would have been inappropriate to be entirely negative in my response to Sunday trading. My positive response was that, if Sunday trading was here to stay and was going to be an important trading day for many retailers, the church needed a presence here too. MetroCentre became the first shopping centre to hold a regular service on Sundays. The service, held in the afternoon and organized using an ecumenical rota, is a chance for the church to say that God is alive and active, the church is here in the malls; come and join us. On a Sunday the centre can have between 40,000 and 100,000 visitors, all the more reason why the church should have a witness on this day.

Initiating a regular service in a place of work was a huge departure for industrial mission. Carol services may have been held in factories, but not services on a regular basis. Within the last few years, however, more regular services are being held in all sorts of places of work and leisure. One part-time retail chaplain, as part of his job description, is obliged to organize a regular act of worship in the shopping centre where he works. At the MetroCentre, the services are lively and shoppers are free to participate in the worship with its 'rent-a-congregation' for a few minutes or stay for the whole service. A number of shoppers have told me touching stories of being made aware of God's presence in their lives through the service. As the Lord's Prayer was being prayed one Sunday a woman shopper was challenged by the line 'Forgive us our trespasses as we forgive those who trespass against us'. She was reminded of her 'unforgiveness' of someone else's trespass. The Lord's Prayer is *always* prayed at these services.

The wider context

Many parish clergy have seen the visiting of places of work within their parish as part of their work of showing that God's church cares for all. Retail chaplaincy complements this work, and there are now over 30 retail chaplains in the UK – mainly part-time, and some voluntary. Many work as retail chaplains within a larger responsibility such as in a town centre, leisure centre, as part of community work, airport or work within large or small stores. Those who are stipendiary are mostly paid by the church and one is paid jointly by the church and commerce. I am a member of the Northumbrian Industrial Mission Team, who help in my ongoing training, provide me with a support group and with whom I liaise for all work-related issues. Many years ago industrial chaplaincy was based around the large, heavy engineering factories. These factories have largely disappeared and industrial chaplains are now involved in diverse areas of work and thus the need for retail chaplains is increasing. Currently many new shopping developments, both out of town and in high streets, are requesting the presence and input of a retail chaplain. It is a request the church should not ignore.

Gaining entry and then what?

Retail chaplains, like many sector ministers, are the guests of the places in which they work. Chaplains need to negotiate entry into stores by contacting the manager or personnel officer. In larger complexes entry is gained via the centre manager or Traders' Association. When I visit, I 'loiter with intent': hanging around, having conversations where I can, sometimes standing alongside shop assistants as they tidy up shelves. I tidy too, I am very good at putting things together in their correct sizes! I also arrange to meet managers and personnel officers and generally strive to be accessible. With many of the larger stores I arrange the time of some visits and this has proved useful, for instance when other staff ask me to see a particular person who would like to talk. It is amazing the range of conversation: family matters; wages; bringing up teenage children; poverty; holidays; football; illness; food and drink; films; cooking; sex; working hours; gardening – the list is endless. I have a rule of not initiating any talk about God, the Bible or the church. Does this mean that these things are not discussed at the MetroCentre? Of course not! They are often spoken of and I am always encouraged by the depth and variety of people's spirituality. It is my experience that God is very much part of people's lives, even if this does not translate into them going to church on a regular basis. If asked, I am able to put those of other faiths in contact with a person from their own religious tradition.

When chaplains visit, through offering friendship, concern and support, they are able to make people conscious of the presence of God. They show that God is interested in the whole of people's lives and is present with them wherever they are. Through their presence they show that the church is not just absorbed in itself. They can offer prayer and comfort (often being asked to pray for someone, to take a relative's funeral or to listen to a trauma). They can offer laughter and hope (rejoicing in new life and hearing of exciting plans made). They can offer a vision or be used as a sounding board. They can be a source of encouragement and understanding, integrity and impartiality. They can also offer an independent Christian opinion; a prophetic voice.

Prophecy

The prophets of the Old Testament were people chosen by God to speak to his people. In the New Testament the Greek word *prophetes* means 'one who speaks for another'. Chaplains, indeed all Christians, can have a prophetic voice. The ancient prophets spoke on behalf of God and others and commented on issues of ethical and social concern. They gave their considered opinions, they commented, they challenged what was happening at the time. Chaplains can do this in a variety of ways. When attending a meeting I am able to question reasons for a particular development or change. I am able to affirm the good that is being done and I am able to point out omissions of care and co-operation. I often meet with managers of various departments and as they tell me of plans and ideas, I am able to comment and help find answers to questions. When visiting, I can respond to individual queries. I encourage all who work at the centre in the support they show to others. I offer, where I can, alternatives to the problems and upsets encountered. One of the frequent topics of conversation is the quality of people's lives. Many feel life is too stressful and they cannot see their way forward. They feel there are too many demands; there is no peace or rest. Often I simply reply 'What's the alternative?', and a meaningful discussion follows. Moses showed the people of Israel an alternative lifestyle to their slavery. We can do the same – though perhaps not so dramatically!

Requests and initiatives

'No, you cannot get married in the MetroCentre!' Notwithstanding the recent changes in English law allowing different places to hold wedding ceremonies, the MetroCentre is not licensed for marriages. Many assume that, because there is a chaplain at the centre, weddings may be held here. Other liturgies (apart from Sunday afternoon worship) do take place, however. One Service of Blessing of wedding rings for a couple who had lost their original pair was delayed somewhat because of theft from the jeweller's shop. When the rings were finally available, the couple asked that the blessing take place in the shop. The service consisted of a Bible reading, a psalm and prayers, and was a very moving occasion for all concerned. The ceremony ended with a glass of champagne, courtesy of the shop owners.

There is a Roman Catholic chapel in the MetroCentre, aesthetically situated in the Mediterranean Village! The Roman Catholic Bishop of Hexham and Newcastle, the Rt Revd Ambrose Griffiths OSB, came to see me with a proposal for a chapel. We agreed three principles. Firstly, the chapel had to be staffed, not only for security reasons, but if people came feeling upset, they would know that someone would be available to them. Secondly, the church would have to pay rent, as any retailer who comes into the centre pays rent and the church cannot be different. Thirdly, the chapel would be open to all, so that people of faith or none would feel welcome there. There are good stories of people finding strength and peace in the chapel. A young worker at the centre who does not attend church felt he needed to talk to God about being forgiven. Time spent in the chapel enabled him to find this forgiveness and a renewed strength.

An exciting development at the MetroCentre is the Youth Information Shop. The shop is a one-stop facility offering support and information for young people aged 14–24. A quarter of all the centre's visitors are in this age group and the shop is the first of its kind in a European shopping mall. The idea began in the Community Education Team of Gateshead Metropolitan Borough Council and, as chaplain, I was asked to approach the Church Commissioners and Capital Shopping Centres for their support. It was willingly given. This venture is now a reality and it was a delight to watch the project blossom; a journey of partnership, co-operation and goodwill between industry and the council, between people of faith and those of none, between business-orientated landlords and community workers. It was a privilege to be involved and a joy to behold. Young people as they mature are now better served by the availability of whatever information and help they need, from within a centre where they already visit.

Communication

From the time the centre was built, the chaplain's office has been housed within the marketing department's offices. Chaplains have always felt part of that team here and valued the link their office location provdes. In the preface of his book *Keep in Touch*, Peter Crumpler writes 'The church in Britain has a communications problem. It fails to communicate to most people, most of the time. It is seen as irrelevant, out-of-touch and old-fashioned, and church-going as a minority interest. Yet surveys show that many people still believe both in God and in a moral code. But these same people see no place in their lives for the church.'[2] In the first chapter of the book Crumpler looks at the way Jesus communicated, and from this says that modern communicators should:

- Know what you want to communicate.
- Know with whom you want to communicate.
- Make sure the message is clearly received.

Many working in marketing would agree with these three principles. When I was newly appointed, whenever there was a media inquiry about the chaplain and the centre, one of the marketing team was alongside to help me focus my response. I learnt to know my message and express it in a concise way. 'Keep it simple' is a marketing motto. In response to the question 'Just exactly what do you do?', I learnt to give a clear and succinct answer lasting 30 seconds. Said with enthusiasm and a smile it gives the questioner an overview of my job. My answer consists of:

- I am there for those who work at MetroCentre.
- I offer an independent voice and opinion on all sorts of issues at all levels.
- I communicate to the church and other secular bodies about the issues of retail.

As well as communicating with words, we also communicate non-verbally. A look, a stance, a gesture or body movement can indicate opinion as much as by what is said. It is important that we get our words and actions right when we communicate. For many in chaplaincy, there is the pressure of having to communicate exactly what we want to say at the first meeting, as this may be the only meeting. I am thankful that my office is located in the marketing department; I may not be perfect in my communication but I have learnt a lot and continue to try to put this into practice.

The future

Shopping will always be a part of our lives and increasingly it will seen as a leisure activity. Depending on lifestyle and income, we will spend varying amounts of time shopping. The job of a retail worker can be very satisfying and rewarding. Many people want to be of service to others in the retail trade, but it can be frustrating and stressful dealing with difficult people and situations, and the working hours can be long and tedious. 'Out-of-town' shopping centres have increasingly longer opening hours to accommodate consumer demand and many of the workers in such centres are part-time. The future promises a complexity of issues to understand and situations to appreciate.

Retail chaplaincy is a part of the church which is available to people where parochial ministry is not. As the church faces up to economic realities, parochial clergy numbers are falling whilst sector ministries seem to be expanding. There is the question of who should pay for this new work. The mission of the church has to be seen in a wider context other than that of 'bottoms on pews'. The mission of the church has to be *both* parish based and economy based. 'Who will listen to us if you're not here?' one worker asked me. Retail chaplaincy is now firmly established – pray God that that worker never finds the answer to her question.

Notes

1 Mike Starkey, *Born to Shop* (London: Monarch, 1994).
2 Peter Crumpler, *Keep in Touch* (London: Scripture Union, 1989).

13

Schools

David Lindsay

The church and schools

The link between the church and education in England is an ancient and strong link. For centuries a Christian ethos has underpinned much of the work of the education of the nation's young. In the nineteenth century especially, much of the philanthropic work of the church and individual Christians was to establish or refound state and private schools. Although most of the schools were of Anglican foundation or influence (inspired by examples such as Thomas Arnold of Rugby and Nathaniel Woodward and his corporation of schools to educate the middle classes), there were a number of institutions founded by Roman Catholic orders or by Nonconformist churches. Because of the clerical monopoly in the universities, until the last few years of the nineteenth century almost all the masters in the (Anglican) grammar and private schools were men in holy orders. There were a number of contributing factors in this rebirth of the importance of education in the nineteenth century; the century was one of colonialism and foreign rule, requiring well-educated, if not well-trained, administrators, and it was a time of religious fervour and pious expression. This background in which educational expansion took place has been described as expressing the ideal of 'Godliness and good learning'.[1]

Why school chaplaincy?

Why on earth should I be a school chaplain? I first asked myself this question when, towards the end of my first curacy in a large parish in the north-east of England, I was offered the job of chaplain to a fairly well-known, and thoroughly traditional, English public school in the Home Counties. I was flattered, since the initiative had come from the school rather than from me, but I had little hesitation in declining the offer. After all, I associated such schools with privilege, wealth, affected accents and conservatism; here was I, a grammar-school educated northerner and not known for being a reactionary. Furthermore, I believed that the most appropriate form of ministry for me to move on to would be university chaplaincy. I explained all this to the wise priest who was at that time my spiritual director, and of whose views on matters both theological and political I was fairly confident. His reply surprised me. 'You must make up your own mind, of course', he said, 'but I've known far more people acknowledge a lasting debt to their school chaplain than to the chaplain of their university.' Twenty-five years on, having duly worked first as a university chaplain and then, for the last 17 years, as a school chaplain, I think I understand what he meant; and the memory of his words has sustained me during those times when I have wondered quite what a person like me is doing in a place like this. I am still thoroughly in favour of state education (my four children have received first-class schooling at the local comprehensive), and I still have considerable misgivings about the ethics of independent education. The fact is, however, that whatever I or anybody else think about independent schools, for the foreseeable future they are here to stay; and I have no doubt whatsoever that the people who constitute their membership – both pupils and staff – are as much in need of the gospel as anyone. Life as a school chaplain has not always been easy or comfortable, but I believe that through it I have been presented with many opportunities to make a lasting difference to thousands of people's lives.

Background

While there are chaplains of private day schools and chaplains of state schools, the majority of school chaplains work in schools broadly similar to the one whose offer of work I declined in 1973 – that is to say, independent boarding schools with a strong sense of history and tradition. Bearing in mind that many (most?) of these schools are of specifically Christian foundation, it is not surprising that the chaplain generally enjoys an important, indeed a central, role, in some ways analogous to that of a parish priest. She symbolizes and provides a focus for a Christian presence in the school. She will have at her disposal a chapel – often one of the school's most imposing buildings – and hers is the responsibility of determining and organizing what happens in it. This will include Sunday and daily worship, which in many cases is still compulsory. Thus the chaplain has the delicate task of ministering regularly to congregations, the majority of whose members are indifferent to the claims of the Christian – or any – religion, and would far sooner be elsewhere. Bearing this in mind, the chaplain will be well advised to make sure that a range of services at which attendance is *voluntary* is also on offer; for example, Compline, informal Eucharists and Taizé worship. Hopefully the chaplain will thus be able to nurture the faithful; and, of course, Confirmation preparation plays an important part in this.

The chaplain will be expected to be a friend and guide to all who seek her out, be they students or staff (teaching or support staff), and she perhaps comes most fully into her own when the school faces the ultimate crises of life and death. While it would be foolish, and indeed dangerous, for any chaplain to claim a monopoly of pastoral care, and while she should fiercely resist the temptation to regard any pupils as 'hers', there is nevertheless a uniqueness about her position which may well result in people (be they pupils or staff) entrusting her with their pain and mess, to a degree that they would not find possible with anyone else. For, while she must be loyal to the school, especially since it pays her salary (which, like the holidays, is undeniably one of the attractions of the job!), she owes another, and greater, loyalty to the gospel. This can enable her, sometimes at least, to sit fairly lightly to the mores and shibboleths of the institution, and to exercise an almost prophetic role as she reminds both colleagues and pupils of the world that lies beyond the playing fields. It is, for example, the particular responsibility of the chaplain to remind such privileged individuals as her pupils that from those to whom much has been given much will be expected. To this end, many chaplains are actively involved in community service and other consciousness-raising activities; for example, I helped to set up our school's Amnesty International Group, and over many years took boys on a weekly visit to a large hospital for those with a mental handicap. Many school chaplains respond vigorously to the challenges posed by such reports as *Faith in the City* on urban priority areas; raising, not simply money, but also awareness.

In one important respect, school chaplaincy differs from most other forms of sector ministry. Hospital chaplains are not doctors; army chaplains do not fight; most university chaplains are not dons; but almost all school chaplains teach, and a good many (myself included) are Heads of Departments. As well as making obvious incursions into one's time and energy, the teaching role can create tensions; the priest and pastor in me sees that young Vincent is a troubled and angry soul who needs tea and sympathy, but as his religious studies teacher I find him a pain in the neck for whom a detention is long overdue! Especially in a day school, there is always the risk that the chaplain may be seen as, and may indeed become, simply a teacher in a dog-collar. However, this need not happen, and if the chaplain is able to live with the tension, it can be a creative one. The great advantage of the teaching role is that one is exposed to the ungodly as much as to the godly; furthermore, through sweating it out at the chalk-face, one's ministry is well and truly 'earthed'. As a university chaplain, I could choose whom to be with – and whom to avoid; when the bell rings for period one, it's the second form, whether I (or they!) like it or not. Only God knows what seeds can grow from such encounters.

An unusual chaplaincy

'I have to warn you', said the Headmaster who appointed me to my present post in 1980, 'that this is a pretty ungodly school. Mind you', he added with a twinkle in his eye, 'I've been in a few godly schools, and they can be hell!' I now work as chaplain and Head of Religious Studies to the Haberdashers' Aske's school, Elstree. The school was founded just over three hundred years ago through the charity of Robert Aske, Master of the Worshipful Company of Haberdashers; but it is only in modern times that it has emerged as one of north London's foremost independent day schools. Despite having no boarders, 'Habs' (as the school is usually known) attracts pupils from across a remarkably wide geographical area; a fleet of buses brings them in in the morning and takes them home at night. The school is characterized by busyness, enterprise, hard work and success – the success taking many forms. We are not an academic sweatshop; our boys play hard as well as work hard. But, as our headmaster acknowledged in a recent newspaper interview, they are rarely still and rarely quiet. In many ways, the school is a stimulating and exciting place in which to work; such highly articulate and able pupils make lively company and can be very rewarding to teach. But there is a darker side, and a price that has to be paid for the success and achievement. All too often we are overcompetitive, and seek not excellence – which is attainable – but perfection, which is not. All too often, too many of our pupils are dominated by an anxious fear – sometimes amounting to hatred – of fellow-pupils whom they perceive as rivals, and by a veritable dread of failure. The word 'arrogant' is quite often applied to our pupils; but the arrogance is but a thin veil covering insecurity and self-doubt. A visiting Franciscan friar, who told the entire school that all he could say to them was that God loved them, gained an immediately attentive audience!

This simple example reminds me of what I am sure is my most important function: namely, to preach the gospel of undeserved and unlimited love and acceptance to an institution that runs on a doctrine of justification by works. Again and again I find myself saying – in assemblies, in chapel, in the classroom and in one-to-one encounters – that we do not have to be perfect, that we all fail (and go on failing), that it is all right to fail and that, however impressive our achievements, it is who we *are*, rather than what we have *achieved*, that is the one truly unique thing that we have to offer. This message is, as far as I am concerned, very close to the heart of the Christian gospel, and I preach it daily – not least to myself – but often in ways that are implicit rather than explicit; for Haberdashers' is far from being, in the traditional sense, a Christian school. About a third of our pupils are Jewish, and we have a considerable – and increasing – number of Asian boys, many of them Hindu, but also including Jains, Muslims, Christians, Sikhs, Buddhists (and even, very occasionally, Jews). It is usually the case that in any one class there will be at least four, and sometimes as many as six, religions represented. Given that our approach to the teaching of Religious Studies is firmly based on a pluralist multi-faith approach, such religious diversity creates excellent opportunities for learning at first hand what it means to be a Jew, a Hindu and so on. I believe that an important part of my role as chaplain is to encourage the school's varied faith communities to explore and deepen their identity; and it is a source of considerable satisfaction to me that we now have a Christian Eucharist in the chapel, a Jewish assembly led by a visiting Rabbi, and Hindu, Muslim and Sikh assemblies led by senior pupils of these faiths, all happening at the same time each week. The task of planning and conducting these assemblies is one which the leaders take with admirable seriousness; and it is interesting to note that several pupils attend gatherings of faiths other than their own fairly regularly. It is by no means unusual, for example, for me to find myself giving a blessing to a Jew or a Hindu while administering communion.

One of the great advantages of day school chaplaincy is that the chapel, rather than being a vast cathedral-like structure all too often associated with compulsion and resistance, can be a fairly small, intimate and quiet place – perhaps more like a modern hospital chapel – where all are welcome, but nobody attends unless they so wish. As I have no set Sunday duties, I am sometimes invited to preach in more traditional school chapels; after attempting to tell the good news to serried ranks of bored young people determined to remain bored (because they have no option but to be there), I have always come home deeply thankful for the chapel at Haberdashers'. It is a large and beautiful room in the seventeenth century house which forms the administrative centre of the school. It is, as I let all new boys know when I show them where the chapel is, the one place in a busy and noisy school where one can always be guaranteed peace and quiet. There are regular events for committed Christians – a weekly Eucharist (currently attended by about 80 pupils), Lent groups, Confirmation groups (we have an annual Confirmation Service) and occasional services such as our very popular candle-light Advent Carol Service. Other events in chapel attract boys of all faiths and none – for example a weekly meeting for silent meditation, and an extremely popular 'Rich Man/ Poor Man' lunch in Christian Aid week. Furthermore, it is gratifying to realize that all kinds of unlikely pupils – and colleagues – do drop in to the chapel from time to time; at the moment a devout Muslim pupil regularly says his prayers there. I wonder how many other school chaplains could open the doors of their chapel and hear the sound of whispered Arabic from behind the altar! From time to time I take members of the chapel congregation away for a day or two – to our diocesan Youth Centre, or to go on retreat in rural Essex or to a Franciscan friary in Dorset. These visits are very popular, and give us all the opportunity to deepen our Christian commitment and to know one another rather better than the fast and furious school day allows. By no means all of the boys who attend chapel regularly come from churchgoing families; I do what I can to encourage them to forge links with their local churches (for example, by requiring Confirmation candidates to interview their parish priest), but there is never any guarantee that this will happen. Nevertheless, a seed has been sown . . . hopefully.

Whilst attendance in chapel is always voluntary, assemblies are for all, unless parents exercise their statutory right of withdrawal (in practice, this never happens). In such a multi-faith community it would be quite inappropriate to regard assemblies as Christian acts of worship, but I do believe that they are valuable occasions, when it is possible to move some pupils at least towards a deeper awareness of life's spiritual dimension. One interesting consequence of the increased Asian intake has been a very much more open and accepting attitude to matters spiritual, which seems to have spread to the non-Asians, even those convinced of their unbelief. The outright rejection and mockery of religion, which was commonplace in 1980, rarely happens now, nor is it considered 'sad' to be taking religious studies at A level, or applying to read theology at university. So while it remains true, in some ways, that Haberdashers' is a pretty ungodly school, it would also be true to say that it is a school in which religion is alive and well, albeit of no one fixed abode!

Conclusion: useful anachronisms

At a school chaplains' conference which I attended in the mid-1980s, one of the guest speakers was David Jenkins, then Bishop of Durham. As always, he was on splendid, sparkling form. One thing that he said in particular keeps coming back to me, and – like my one-time spiritual director's comments – is a source of encouragement and reassurance. 'Public schools', said Bishop David, 'are – like bishops – a bit of an anachronism. But the important thing – as I tell myself daily – is to be a *useful* anachronism!' To aim at being a useful anachronism is, surely, not dishonourable; and it may be that the chaplain, in particular, has the task of attempting to ensure that the anachronism in question is as useful as possible. A year or two ago, the senior chaplain at one of Britain's leading public schools suggested that the employment of public school chaplains could be justified by pointing to the important positions which members of the chaplain's flocks would go on to hold in society. This could be a dangerous argument, and I can understand the wrath it provoked in some quarters. Jesus himself, after all, did not choose clever or influential men to be his disciples, and appears not to have been altogether the sort of person we tend to look for when appointing our head boys or girls! Nevertheless, it is surely the case that a privileged, articulate and able young person who has been (in whatever way) exposed to the gospel is much to be preferred to one who has not; and if a chaplain has helped to achieve this, then I do not believe that her time has been wasted. Even an anachronism may help change the world.

Notes

1   This background is described further in David Newsome, *Godliness and Good Learning: Four Studies on a Victorian Ideal* (London: John Murray, 1961).

14

Seafarers

Bill Down

History of the church's involvement in maritime ministry

The origins of ministry to seafarers lie in the ministry of Jesus himself: he based his ministry in a port city, Capernaum; he chose Peter, one of four fishermen among his twelve apostles, to be the rock on which to build his church; and he demonstrated dramatically his authority over the winds and the sea. In the earliest days of the church, St Paul frequently travelled by sea as he proclaimed the gospel throughout the Mediterranean, and his faith and composure made a profound impact on the terrified crew of the ship carrying him to his trial in Rome when they were shipwrecked on the coast of Malta. The practical care of the Maltese for the survivors set an example for future ministry to seafarers.

From New Testament times until the end of the eighteenth century there were a number of outstanding individual instances of maritime ministry. St Columba and his monks evangelized the Hebrides from their tiny frail boats and a few monasteries provided sanctuary for sick or injured sailors. Some clergy asked God's blessing on new ships at the start of long voyages. There is a record of an English naval chaplain in the tenth century. In the sixteenth century King Henry VIII established Trinity House in London: it was a guild of 'shipmen and mariners' dedicated to work for the glory of God and the prosperity and welfare of the nation's shipping industry. The Governor of the Company of Merchant Adventurers, Sebastian Cabot, instructed his captains that the services of Morning and Evening Prayer were to be read daily on every ship. St Francis Xavier was a brilliant voyage chaplain. St Vincent de Paul improved conditions for galley slaves. John Newton, a slave-ship captain, came to faith through the influence of another Christian captain, and later became a Church of England priest and wrote a number of hymns, including 'Amazing Grace'.

Early in the nineteenth century the church began, in a more structured way, to take seriously its ministry to seafarers. In the reformed churches in Britain and North America permanent ministries to seafarers were established and seafarers' centres built. The non-denominational British and International Sailors' Society originated in 1818. The Anglican Missions to Seamen was founded in 1856, bringing together and formalizing already existing work. The Lutheran churches in Europe, too, established national ministries in the second half of the century.

In the twentieth century this establishment of ministry to seafarers continued. In 1922 the Roman Catholic Apostleship of the Sea came into being, formally recognizing a growing apostolate and bringing a broader dimension to maritime ministry. In 1969 the International Christian Maritime Association was formed, with the aim of promoting and enabling collaboration among all Christian organizations ministering to seafarers, and it has had much success.

A seafarer's life

In order to understand and appreciate the church's ministry in the maritime world it is helpful to know what a seafarer's life involves. Life at sea is lonely. Seafarers can be away from home for long periods of time, and miss their families and friends. They miss a regular social life with people other than those with whom they work. Leaving home for long trips becomes increasingly painful. Life at sea can be boring. Out of sight of land, one stretch of water looks much like another. Routine duties can become tedious. Constructive use of leisure time can be challenging when the ship is pitching, rolling or vibrating at speed – even writing a letter can be an impossible task. Life at sea has a real element of physical danger. Every year more than 100 vessels of 500 or more gross tonnes are lost at sea through bad weather, collisions, fire, uncharted hazards or other causes. In 1996 105 ships were lost and 1,190 passengers and crew died.

Life at sea can also be very satisfying. It is good to travel widely and to experience different cultures, customs and food, or to be a trusted member of a well-run ship. Learning to cope with the sea in all its moods is stimulating and many gain strength from being part of the great fellowship of the sea – an intangible, unarticulated, but very real bond – linking all seafarers in spontaneous willing assistance to fellow sailors in trouble or danger. But the pressures of shipboard life today, coupled with short stays in port and the relentless requirement to meet deadlines at all costs, have eroded job satisfaction to some extent.

However, seafarers do not spend all their lives at sea. In port they often face testing situations. Many of them naturally want a break from shipboard life – but the ship may be berthed a long way from the nearest centre of population; there may be no public transport; taxis may be too expensive; they may need to obtain local currency; they may not understand or speak the local language; they may want to telephone home, or do some urgent shopping. Activities which residents take for granted can be massive problems for seafarers. Similarly, unfamiliarity with the port where they have arrived may well present dangers for them. Dockside bars abound with thieves, muggers, drug dealers and others intent on parting the unwary from their money, and prostitutes may carry sexually transmitted diseases. There are real hazards for the innocent or naïve.

Home life is another factor which seafarers must learn to deal with when they go to sea. Unmarried seafarers may feel the need to establish a secure shore base, whilst married seafarers will miss the joys of family life, such as watching the daily development of little children and bonding with them. Whether single or married, establishing and maintaining domestic responsibilities can cause real heartache. Uncertainty of employment has always been an element of seafaring. The availability of jobs depends on many complex factors including relations between nations, healthy patterns of trade, demand and supply, and the cost of labour, all of which are constantly changing.

The maritime scene today

The process of evolution in the maritime world has accelerated rapidly during the last two centuries. Wooden-hulled sailing ships gave way to steel-hulled steam, diesel or nuclear-powered vessels. Since the Second World War, container and roll on/roll off ships, huge bulk carriers and ultra large tankers, rig supply tenders, Liquid Natural Gas carriers and other specialist vessels have been introduced. Passenger liners have disappeared from the scene, and cruise ships and sophisticated ferries have multiplied. Ships now turn round more swiftly in port and cargo handling is faster and safer. Conditions for seafarers on modern ships are generally very good – there are excellent navigation and weather aids, the accommodation and leisure facilities are first class and there is often a small well-equipped medical centre or hospital.

There is, however, a small but significant number of sub-standard ships. These are often old vessels run by unscrupulous operators who register the ships under a flag of convenience and ignore or flout accepted standards of safety and operation.[1] These owners fail to maintain the ships properly. They allow debts to accumulate, and then re-register the ships under different names and in different places to avoid their responsibilities. They often fail to meet their contractual obligations to the crews. Irresponsible ownership is one reason why ship losses each year remain unacceptably high.

Since the 1960s there has been a steep decrease in the numbers of seafarers from developed countries, and a rapid increase in the numbers from developing countries. At present some two-thirds of the world's merchant seafarers are Asian – it is much less expensive for ship owners to employ seafarers from developing countries than from affluent ones. Another problem is the significant number of people who, in the hope of obtaining work in another country, of escaping political oppression or returning home when attempts to work elsewhere have failed, now stow-away on deep-sea ships.

Piracy (armed robbery at sea) remains a perennial problem on the maritime scene, despite determined efforts to eradicate it. It is common in Asia and South America, and also to a lesser degree in other parts of the world. In 1996 official sources reported 175 instances of piracy, although this figure does not represent the full picture, since some cases are not reported.[2] It is disturbing to note that the incidence of piracy is increasing rather than decreasing.

Strenuous efforts are being made in many parts of the world by intergovernmental bodies, international trade, labour and welfare organisations, insurance companies and national governments to raise safety standards throughout the industry and to remunerate seafarers adequately. The church is deeply involved in the day-to-day lives of seafarers and of the industry as a whole, and its role and contribution in this area is highly valued and appreciated.

The nature of the church's ministry to seafarers

From the beginning of the nineteenth century, when the churches began to give serious attention to maritime ministry, the clergy and lay people engaged in it clearly understood that their ministry to seafarers must be relevant and appropriate if it was to be effective. They soon observed and noted the nature of the lives of seafarers and their multinational, multicultural, multilingual and multi-faith backgrounds. They recognized the need to minister to the whole person, to provide a comprehensive service to seafarers and to make readily available to seafarers whatever they might legitimately want or need, as well as what the churches themselves wanted to offer. They realized too that they had a ministry to those who make decisions affecting the lives of seafarers, and to all who earn their living on or through the sea.

There are a number of qualities to note about the church's ministry to seafarers.

Practical and pastoral
Priority is given to visiting seafarers on their ships. Modern ships do not stay long in port and shore leave is not always convenient or possible. The visits of

the chaplains, ordained and lay, provide a much appreciated opportunity to share concerns with somebody reliable and trustworthy. If seafarers are planning shore leave the chaplain can often arrange transport from and back to the ship – a godsend when the ship is at a remote berth or the weather is extreme. In 1996 more than 300,000 seafarers were given help with transport by the staff of The (Anglican) Missions to Seamen.

Priority is also given to providing well-equipped centres where seafarers of all races, ranks, religions and ideologies are welcomed. These centres offer a wide range of facilities and services, such as a chapel, shop, bar, canteen or restaurant, currency exchange, recreational activities, television, videos, telephones, reading material and sometimes swimming pools. It is not unusual for a busy seafarer's centre to put through 30–40 telephone calls a day to connect seafarers with their families. If the news from home is worrying, the chaplain can usually arrange immediate action through the worldwide network of chaplains and clergy. The size, location, trading patterns and climate of the port determine what facilities are provided. The centres are well used – in 1996 900,000 seafarers visited the 104 centres of the Missions to Seamen. As well as the assistance given at port, chaplains also visit seafarers in hospital or gaol, arrange sporting activities or tours to places of interest.

Evangelistic

It would be wrong to see maritime ministry as almost exclusively practical and pastoral. The churches have always seen the primary objective of their ministry as the total well-being of seafarers – spiritual and moral as well as physical. Their calling is to proclaim Jesus Christ as the Way, the Truth and the Life.

There are particular challenges in witnessing to the Christian faith in the maritime world: language barriers, shortness of contact time, little opportunity to speak on a one-to-one basis and pressure of work are just a few. But challenges also bring opportunities. In its evangelistic outreach to seafarers the church consciously seeks to appeal to every human faculty. The quality of the service it offers prompts questions as to why it is being provided. The striking visual appearance of a seafarers' centre may lift the spirits of visitors and point beyond the present. The ready availability of Bibles in different languages and the dignity and peace of a simple chapel proclaim eternal values. Here flowers, pictures and music can play their part in making people aware of God.

The dedicated lives of individual Christians can also make a great impact. Basic moral integrity, a disciplined lifestyle, a healthy outlook on life underpinned by a deep faith and a respect for others which does not seek to force personal convictions on them: all combine to present a powerful witness to Jesus Christ.

Ecumenical

In 1969 a momentous conference in Rotterdam brought together more than 100 delegates of national and international Christian voluntary organizations serving seafarers. Their purpose was to identify the current needs of seafarers, assess how far these were being met, and determine what more could be done. Those who were present were convinced that the Holy Spirit guided their deliberations. They agreed unanimously that their ministries would be most effective if they were exercised together rather than separately and the International Christian Maritime Association (ICMA) was brought into being. Its aim was to promote inter-confessional collaboration and to speak with one voice on behalf of all its members.

Within ten years there were ecumenical partnerships in many ports all over the world – Antwerp, Brisbane, Buenos Aires, Felixstowe, Hong Kong, Houston, Immingham, Kobe, Lagos, Vancouver and Yokohama were early examples. Where previously several denominations had been operating independently they now came together under one roof. The staff prayed together, planned together and worked together. Collaboration between Anglicans, Lutherans, Roman Catholics and other denominational organizations became a reality. Redundant buildings were sold, releasing money for new work. Today regular international and regional conferences are held under the auspices of ICMA. New ministries are usually undertaken together. The principle of being partners in ministry and guests in each other's buildings is established and accepted. The Churches are 'on course' together.[3]

International

When the reformed churches in Britain and the United States of America began to get involved in maritime ministry it was through local initiatives and local people. In the middle of the nineteenth century the newly formed Anglican Missions to Seamen stated its aim as being to promote the spiritual welfare of seafarers at home and abroad, ashore and afloat. By the end of the century it was in action in every continent. Its chaplains were British, and its overseas representation was mainly in ports under British jurisdiction. Working along similar lines, the non–denominational British and Foreign Sailors' Society was established in 1833. The American Seamen's Friend Society sent a number of missionaries to overseas ports from 1830 onwards. When the Roman Catholic Apostleship of the Sea was formally commissioned by the Pope in 1922 it operated on a diocesan basis, with the bishops appointing clergy to this ministry. Many of the chaplains were indigenous priests and this added an extra dimension to the overall chaplaincy picture.

From the 1960s the Missions to Seamen increasingly encouraged the worldwide Anglican Communion to assume more responsibility for maritime ministry. Many Provinces appointed Liaison Bishops, who in turn appointed local clergy to port ministries. A resolution adopted by the 1988 Lambeth Conference of Bishops formally acknowledged the Missions to Seamen as the outreach of the Anglican Communion to the seafarers of the world. Its ministry was thereby recognized as being truly international.

A typical example of the international co-operation of maritime ministry was the chaplaincy team at Dar es Salaam in Tanzania in the late 1980s: it included a Japanese Anglican bishop as Senior Chaplain, a Tanzanian Assistant Chaplain, a French Roman Catholic chaplain and an English lay reader/Club Manager. In Vancouver in the same period there was an Irish Anglican Senior Chaplain, a Canadian Roman Catholic chaplain and Presbyterian chaplains from Korea and Taiwan. They all worked together wonderfully.

Prophetic

In this context prophecy means speaking God's word for a particular situation at a particular time. Christians believe that all people are made in the image of God and are of equal value and importance to him. As equals we should treat each other with dignity, respect and justice. But from earliest times some nations, groups of people or individuals have sought to exploit others and the maritime world is no exception to this. Throughout history there have been courageous men and women who have opposed injustice, oppression, greed and exploitation. The Old Testament prophets fiercely denounced such behaviour. Our Lord Jesus Christ gave his life drawing humanity back to himself, and brave Christians have followed in his steps.

The maritime world today faces significant injustice and exploitation of seafarers. Many seafarers from developing countries get a raw deal: from unscrupulous ship operators who fall behind in paying wages; on some flag-of-convenience ships which are unsafe because of faulty equipment or lack of proper maintenance; because of inadequate contracts of service or from manning agents who exploit their desperate need for work.

The church cannot remain silent in such circumstances and it does not – it speaks in many ways through many different groups and individuals. In 1985 the ICMA held a plenary conference in the Philippines and focused attention on the plight of Filipino seafarers on overseas-registered ships; the Cardinal Archbishop of the Philippines himself presented the conference's concerns to the government of the Philippines. The Center for Seafarers' Rights in New York came into being to represent seafarers and ensure justice for them, and individual chaplains all over the world and of all denominations are ready to speak out for seafarers with problems. The church's voice is powerful and respected in the maritime world – it speaks God's word in today's situation and it is too strong to be ignored.

The contribution of maritime ministry to the life of the church

The rich and varied insights and experience of those who have served in the maritime ministry of the churches have much of value to contribute to the life of the church as a whole. For more than a quarter of a century the churches have been working together in partnership under one roof in many ports. This has led to deep and lasting friendships between clergy and lay people of different traditions, nationalities, races and cultures. It has involved regular daily planning of joint operations. It has called for humility, patience, tolerance and a sense of humour. It has been underpinned by commitment to Jesus Christ and worshipping together. It has led to greater understanding of each other's Christian traditions and of the Christian faith itself. This is a ministry of living ecumenism.

The challenge to proclaim the gospel effectively in a multifaceted international setting requires regular analysis and assessment of progress, imaginative thinking, sensitivity towards other people, a flexible approach and a willingness to take the initiative to meet people. This is a ministry of imaginative evangelism.

Two centuries of deep involvement with the shipping world in all its diversity and at every level have won for the church a high level of admiration, respect, affection and gratitude. Its contribution is highly valued. This is a ministry of true mission.

Finally, maritime ministry is a ministry ready to face and tackle change and progress. It is forward thinking. The writer of this chapter is grateful for 27 years of richly satisfying ministry, joyfully shared with colleagues of many traditions.

Notes

1 'Flag of convenience' is the practice of registering a ship in a country other than the one in which it is owned. This is often done to obtain favourable tax concessions, to avoid the stringent safety standards of the country of ownership or to escape the attentions of trades unions over conditions of employment.
2 Statistics taken from the 1996 *Annual Report on Piracy* of the International Maritime Bureau. The IMB is a division of the International Chamber of Commerce.
3 For a fuller history of the churches' ecumenical involvement see Bill Down, *On Course Together* (Norwich: Canterbury Press, 1989).

15

Universities

Giles Legood

In this chapter we will examine the history of higher education chaplaincy in the United Kingdom, discuss some theological themes which may underpin chaplaincy and see how what is believed about God and the world shapes the way chaplaincy operates. Because university chaplaincy is so diverse (chaplains work alone or in teams, on a single campus or on a range of sites, part-time or full-time, as members of the university staff or as guests sent by the church), this chapter will not make any claims to universal truth or suggest that the model presented is to be regarded as normative for all university chaplaincy. The theological reflection it offers may however resonate with some of the experiences of chaplains working in sectors other than the university.

Historical experience

According to current statistics there are over 400 chaplains, some full-time, some part-time, working in 180 universities, Oxbridge colleges, church colleges and other colleges of higher education in the UK. In addition there are also a number of non-stipendiary clergy working in the sector in a chaplaincy role. The variety of all these institutions (henceforth in this chapter generically called 'universities') and the variety of the methods that are used to support the chaplains are reflected in the host of different ministerial models which are worked and lived out. This variety comes, in no small part, from the different histories and expectations from both individual institutions and individual chaplains alike.

There has always traditionally been a strong presence of clergy in the colleges of Oxford and Cambridge. A number of these colleges can claim to have been founded before the Reformation and some were originally monastic foundations. Until the nineteenth century, Fellows, that is those responsible for the decision-making and teaching in these places, were required to be unmarried Anglican clergy. In such an environment it was not always found necessary to have a particular person designated as 'chaplain' because, with the ancient tutorial system, most colleges felt that the pastoral welfare of their students was already well met. As regulations regarding the necessity for Fellows to be unmarried and later for them to be clerks in Holy Orders were changed, so too attitudes of colleges towards appointing chaplains changed.

Elsewhere in England the pattern of chaplaincy provision was also piecemeal. At the University of London (the first institution to break the Oxford/Cambridge hegemony) chaplaincy and religious affiliation was a contentious issue. University College London was founded in 1826 specifically to dispense with the need for students and staff to be members of the established church or indeed to be of any religious affiliation at all. It built no chapel and appointed no chaplain. King's College London on the other hand, founded just three years later, was an Anglican foundation, appointed a Dean and chaplain and saw itself in direct opposition to 'the godless institution of Gower Street.'[1]

In considering the history of university chaplaincy in England, the period of greatest significance is the time immediately after the Second World War. Previously the church's involvement in universities outside Oxbridge was largely restricted to financial provision for student accommodation. In 1947, however, the Church of England established a Council for Education and set about broadening the involvement by setting up a working party of academics to look at promoting the church's work in universities. In its report this working party made the recommendation that the best way of forwarding the church's work in this area was the provision of chaplains who had some official status. Negotiations then took place within the church as to how funding could be provided for this recommendation. From 1955 the Church Assembly set aside money for the work of chaplaincies in universities. At the same time a 'Chaplaincies' Advisory Group' was set up by the Council for Education, to co-ordinate chaplaincy work and to provide support for individual chaplains. This Group consisted of chaplains, academics, Board members and a repre-sentative from the Board of Finance, and continued to meet until 1985, since when its work has been continued by a full-time, stipendiary, ordained Secretary for Higher Education working within the Church of England's Board of Education. The Board defines one of its tasks as making a contribu-tion by 'Helping the church build up its ministry in Higher Education by means of the advisory, liaison, and representative services to chaplaincy work in HE already established'.[2]

The size of the task undertaken by the Church of England and its ecumenical partners in these post-war years was enormous. In 1952 there were just eight chaplains in universities outside Oxbridge; by 1985 chaplaincies were established in every university, polytechnic and church college in the country. Indeed the expansion was even more pronounced than these figures indicate. Of the original eight posts just three were filled by full-time clergy, of the others four were filled by parish clergy and one by a cathedral Canon.

The church's expansion into higher education was of course driven by the massive expansion of higher education itself since the war. In the academic year 1954/55 there were 82,000 students in higher education; by 1978/79 this figure was 225,000 and in 1996/97 it was 1,750,000. Put another way, the figures are even more startling; 20 years ago one in every seven 18-year-olds was in higher education, today it is one in three. The Dearing Report on higher education of July 1997 recommended that this expansion be allowed to continue even further. It remains to be seen in the UK whether the newly introduced notion of students paying a contribution towards their fees will have a significant impact upon this expansion.

This then is the scene in which contemporary university chaplaincy is set. Massive expansion in higher education in the post-war period was matched by an equal commitment on the church's part to be involved in a fundamental way in this part of human life. A university education itself was becoming a significant life experience for more and more people and the church was resolved to be involved in this.

Theological reflection on chaplaincy

Theologians in the developing world have in recent years emphasized the importance of the context in which ministry takes place. Because of the context of their environment, university chaplains engage continually with the structures which constitute, in part, the university. In order to engage in a way which is appropriate a chaplain may have a theology which sees human-kind and the natural world as interdependent in God's creation. All are to be transformed and redeemed together. On the one hand, humans are important as individuals because they have a unique relationship to God (made in God's image and likeness – Genesis 1:26), and because they are the agents of God's creativity in the world. On the other hand, the structures of the world have a significance of their own, because they are part of God's creation, a creation which involves the goodness of all (Genesis 1:31: 'And God saw all that he had made, and behold, it was very good'). A theology of ministry should therefore be concerned both with the individual and with the world in which the individual is set.

This concern for both the individual and the world needs to be properly balanced. We can see, for instance, that an over-emphasis on one side of the equation could be to the detriment of the other. One chaplain might see her ministry as being directed to changing lives of individual students and staff through the gospel, and may believe that if enough individual lives are changed then the institution itself will change. She might alternatively feel that the institution will never change to any significant degree and that therefore individuals need to be saved out of the world (this could lead to a ghetto mentality). Another chaplain, concerned more with 'the world', might be excessively interested in the structures of the organization and give great importance to the task of bringing the gospel to bear though the processes of committees or group work, in which she seeks to show that chaplains are willing to get their hands dirty. Both these can be seen as caricatures to clarify the point being made but they highlight the precariousness of the balance to be achieved. One cannot adequately minister to individuals without having a real concern for the systems in which they live and work, nor should one minister and talk of redeeming the institution without being aware that it is largely individuals who constitute the institution.[3] In a university environment where outcomes are preferred to process, a theology of creation can teach us that our priority ought to be the other way round.

In practice it is unavoidable that chaplains will lay stress on some particular aspect of ministry. Much will depend upon chaplains' theology and gifts. Some will have talents which point them towards a ministry with individuals, while others will have talents which equip them for specific work with groups or structures. A ministry which fails to work both for the salvation of the individual and for the world in which she lives will fall short of being a fully adequate Christian ministry. A number of chaplains have found it helpful to identify themselves as co-learners with those in the learning environment in which they work. Through either participating in a formal study themselves or organizing informal courses for others, they are able to show in a powerful way a concern with individuals and groups.

Much of the theology we have examined so far stems from the creation myths of the Old Testament. Here creation is seen as intrinsically good, something to be celebrated as it is from God. The life and death of Jesus contribute something further in looking at theology which might inform university chaplaincy. Christian ministry takes its stance from the life of Jesus, who came not to be served but to serve (Mark 10:25). Through Jesus being in human form, God identified with humanity in a new way. This theology of the incarnation is recognized (if somewhat sporadically) in the New Testament, most notably worked out in John's gospel and in the letters of Paul. Written in the light of the experience of the earliest church, these writings construct a theology where the gap between God and humankind is crossed from the side of God. God, in the human form of Jesus, becomes known to the world and lives a life of sacrifice. In this way the link between God and the world is made in a stronger way than was hitherto known. Before, God was the creator of the world, now, according to the New Testament, God is part of it. In becoming human God also affirms the essential goodness of creation and the essential goodness of humankind. Though not systematically worked out in the New Testament (it took five centuries for a developed Christology to emerge), the notion of incarnation holds that, through Jesus, God is involved in the world of human suffering and demonstrates a commitment to be immersed at an individual, a social and a political level. In a university this incarnational presence ought therefore to witness at a micro level to individuals and groups of individuals, and at a macro level to structures and committees. By getting to know students and staff a chaplain is able to engage at the micro level. At the macro level, one chaplain, at a university committee, was able to question a statement that the university was in the business of educating medical students (she thought rather that they were trained, and a fruitful discussion ensued).

We might ask the question 'Why did God feel it necessary to be known through Jesus?' Traditionally, the church's answer has been that God needed to 'buy back' that which was somehow lost. This idea may owe something to the context of the world of the early church. The Hellenistic world was one of trade, of buying and selling. In the market places goods were sold and purchased; slaves were one of these 'goods'. The writers of the New Testament naturally drew on this experience when reflecting on the nature of what they believed Jesus had done for humanity. Through identifying with human temptations, trials, hopes, suffering and ultimately death, these writers felt that Jesus 'redeemed' humanity (see for example, Ephesians 1:7 and 4:30). For theologians working in English this concept of redemption is closely linked to the word 'atonement' which speaks of the idea of two formerly separated parties now being 'at one'.

It is not hard for us to draw useful material from these thoughts of creation, incarnation and redemption. The essence of university life is the pursuit of knowledge, study. Newman in his famous lectures delivered between 1852 and 1858 and known now as *The Idea of a University* put it thus: 'True enlargement of mind is the power of viewing many things at once as one whole, of referring them severally to their true place in the universal system, of understanding their respective values, and determining their mutual dependence.'[4] In our own day some have argued that there has been a fragmentation of study into different activities and that this needs to be corrected.[5] In the light of what we have previously said, this pursuit of knowledge is, for Christians, a pursuit of understanding about the divinely created world. Indeed, we could go further and say that this study is in itself part of the creative purpose of God. We could say then that part of the theology which lies behind the church's appointments of chaplains in universities 'is to help people see how the world in which they live – the world of learning, science, society and culture – actually comes from God and is to be returned to God'.[6] If this is how the Judaeo-Christian understanding of creation can help us, what of incarnation and redemption?

Ministry is an enterprise which takes place wherever there is a Christian presence. When thinking of chaplaincy it is all too easy to make the mistake of thinking that Christian witness and ministry takes place primarily through those who have been ordained for ministry by the church. Nevertheless, by virtue of her appointment as a Christian chaplain, the chaplain has a special responsibility to be a Christian presence. A university chaplain is to be a public representative of the church and by virtue of her ordination she is to confront the apostolic nature of ministry. In accompanying staff and students in their pursuit of knowledge and in ministering to them in times of joy and need, she is also to be a representative of Christ. Through being in human form, in Christ, God took the human condition seriously and engaged with it at the most fundamental level. By being a Christian presence, whether recognized or not, the chaplain (indeed every Christian in the institution) identifies in a way also shared by Christ in the struggles and joys of human life. Indeed, like the original disciples, some of those with whom the chaplain makes the journey may look back at the meeting and say 'Did our hearts not burn within us while he talked with us on the road?' (Luke 24:32).[7] In this way she may be able to facilitate moments of disclosure as she accompanies people on their journeys.

The language of salvation (redemption) has an important part in the Christian story. However, its meaning is not always clear. In some of the earliest of the Christian scriptures salvation appears to be referred to as a future event in which God will judge the world (see Romans 13:11 or 1 Thessalonians 5:8, for example). In other parts of the New Testament, however, salvation can be seen as a past event by which humanity has already benefited (see Ephesians 2:5 or Romans 8:24, for example). Whichever hermeneutic is applied, however, we can say that salvation is seen as necessary where actions need to be taken in order to restore things to how they should be. In a university setting, indeed in any place where human beings are found, salvation will be necessary because things will not be perfected. In a university setting, where students measure their success by exams results and academic staff measure success by research and publication, it is easy to fall into the error that salvation is achieved by knowledge. Wisdom, healing and wholeness, however, are not so easily achieved. In the current economic climate universities are simply employers and not benevolent 'others' caring for all within them. A chaplain may be in a position to counsel caution about the perfectibility of the individual or institution. A university and its members have a responsibility to influence society for its well-being, not merely for economic success. In order to remind the university, as an institution, of this the chaplain should make a critical discernment of the needs, rather than the desires, of society. This may be hard to do in a culture which has doubled the number of new graduates in the last ten years but has seen its funding cut by 40 per cent over the same period.

Thus far we have seen how the doctrines of creation, incarnation and redemption can inform the chaplain's task. Before we move on to make our final remarks, however, there is a concept which underlies all these – the notion of 'grace'. It is a theological idea which cannot be stressed too much in thinking about chaplaincy.

In the New Testament the word 'grace' refers to God's graciousness towards humankind. It is usually used to denote the special status of those who saw themselves as members of the body of Christ (see 1 Corinthians 12:27, for example). As the thinking and development of doctrine evolved, the early church Fathers later came to talk of grace more as a transformation. This transformation was understood as transforming human life into a godly life. Grace was therefore conceived as a gift from God given to all people. Through this gift people are able to know and love God in a way beyond that of the relationship of creature and Creator. Grace is thus seen as undeserved, but free.

When reflecting on the nature of ministry and the ministry of university chaplaincy in particular, the concept of grace is a very rich theological tool. God's grace in opening a channel of communication between divinity and humanity is essential for the relationship of God with sinners. A chaplain does well to hold this before her in all she does. Because of grace, a relationship is not based on judgement but on forgiveness. A university chaplain saying 'Your sins are forgiven' is a profoundly different discourse from that of counsellors or other welfare workers. In her work in her institution a chaplain should strive to open the channel of communication between the individual and God and between individuals and each other. A chaplain is probably in the unique position of having access to all in the university. No one but the chaplain is able to make such links between academic disciplines and staff. Through her knowledge of personnel from the Vice-Chancellor to the porters, academic staff and administrative staff, full-time young undergraduates and part-time mature postgraduates, a chaplain can see the institution as a whole. In ministry it is not the calling of Christians to judge others but to love others. This love should be unconditional, like the gracious love of God, and should also be free, without hope or expectation of reward. The chaplain's task (and the task of all Christians) is to live this out and to draw others into this deification.

Chaplaincy and the future of higher education

In looking at university chaplaincy we have seen how the theological concepts of creation, incarnation, redemption and grace can all make a significant contribution to informing the task. The doctrine of creation affirms the goodness of the created order and that it is to be celebrated as it is from God. The doctrine of the incarnation affirms the essential goodness of humankind and that God is committed to individual, social and political concerns. The doctrine of redemption teaches us that although perfectibility is not possible we need to strive to restore things to how they should be. Underlying all this is the concept of grace; the concept of forgiveness not judgement, the divine grace which shows us that we are to love others with no expectation or hope of reward.

In a university setting a chaplain needs to think of these implications for her own ministry. She may find it helpful to remember that both for the students and for the staff with whom she ministers much is potential, little is established. Whether pressures of exams or of research come upon the people in her institution, much is unsettling in a university (although for students, as long as they perform in a satisfactory way in assessments they will, at least, know where their lives will be focused for the foreseeable future – the same cannot be said about many in paid employment). Again, in terms of identification, the chaplain might do well to remember the transitory nature of her life and ministry and that of those around her.

As a representative of Christ and with the charge to build up the body of Christ, the chaplain could heed these words, 'To be a congregation means to live out the presence of God and declare it, to be present in God's name in places where life is destroyed, endangered or impaired. Consequently, in the congregation people must feel that the love of God reaches them and that they have been invited to take part in the incarnation of this love for others.'[8] This could serve well as an experience and a theology of university chaplaincy.

Notes

1 See F. M. L. Thompson (ed.), *The University of London and the World of Learning 1836–1986* (London: Hambledon Press, 1990).

2 Jo Linzey (ed.), *The Church of England Year Book 1998* (London: Church House Publishing, 1998), p. 32.

3 This point is well made in the chapter 'Thinking about a city in order to reform it' in Kenneth Underwood, *The Church, the University and the Social Policy* (Middleton, CT: Wesleyan University Press, 1969), vol. 1, pp. 255–69.

4 John Henry Newman, *The Idea of a University* (New Haven: Yale University Press, 1996), p. 99.

5 See, for example, Alasdair MacIntyre, *Three Rival Versions of Moral Enquiry* (London: Duckworth, 1988), pp. 213–36.

6 Daniel Hardy, 'The public nature of theology' (unpublished lecture given at the Higher Education Chaplains' Conference 1994), p. 3.
7 This biblical reference is made by Christopher Moody, 'Students, chaplaincy and pilgrimage', *Theology* LXXXIX (November 1986), p. 447.
8 D. Werner, 'Theological perspectives on congregational renewal' in C. Linn (ed.), *Hear What the Spirit Says to the Churches* (Geneva: WCC Publications, 1994), p. 4.

PART THREE

Further reflection

16

Professional issues

Keith Lamdin

We use the word 'professional' in different ways. Sometimes we use it simply to mean that a footballer (for example) is paid and not just playing in leisure time. In other settings it raises a set of expectations in our minds about whether the job that needs doing will be done well. We expect the person called a professional to be trained to a high standard. We expect them to be authorized and supported by a union or professional body that can vouch for their ability and offer some insurance against malpractice. We expect those people, whether they be a lawyer, builder, doctor, teacher or priest, to be 'good at the job' and able to keep 'up to date'. It is in this latter sense that I want to use the idea of professionalism and focus on three areas. First, I want to look at the development of good practice 'on site'. Secondly, I am interested in how chaplains, while away from the face-to-face contact with 'the site', set about making sense of their experience as sector ministers; and thirdly, I want to think about the need for those in sector ministry and those in the 'sending' and sponsoring institutions (normally the churches) to relate to one another in much more creative ways than seem to have been found so far.

Good practice 'on site'

Listening to the stories of sector ministers, first of all it is obvious that the ability to offer pastoral care to all sorts of people, whether they are clients or providers, prisoners or prison staff, lies at the heart of sector ministry. Secondly, this building of relationship provides a base for the political and prophetic skills of relating across the natural divides within institutions and raising issues that no one else can. A third area is the skill of shaping liturgy, often for those who are unfamiliar with traditional Christian worship. Briefly, I want to look at each of these.

The ability to create and nurture human relationships lies at the heart of all Christian ministry. The parish priest has to build relationships within the expectations of years of accumulated tradition. The baptized, as employees or employers, are caught up in the power structures of the organization, but the chaplain is freed from these structures and anxieties of authority. Visiting the bedside in a hospital ward, the cell of a prisoner, the family of a soldier, sitting in a student bar or 'loitering with intent' in a shopping centre or an airport lounge have widely different settings but need the same human gifts. The need is to listen and offer empathy. There are times when all you can do is wait and say nothing and there are times when a word of encouragement or interpretation is life-changing. There are times when nothing can be done and other times when offering to do something and doing it is the work of the Good Samaritan, and speaks of Christ as clearly as any words. Sometimes it is right to name Christ and offer a prayer. These natural, yet highly skilful, choices weave the tapestry of love and companionship on the human journey.

The way in which the sector ministry fits structurally in the sector opens up another range of opportunities and responsibilities. Whether the minister is paid by the institution as in the military, hospitals, schools and prisons, or paid by the churches, there is, nonetheless, an agreement in almost all institutions receiving chaplaincy, that the minister will have a freedom to roam and build relationships in all parts of the institution. This is not so very different from being a parish priest but it can be focused in quite stark ways. There are, of course, differing implications for a chaplain with an officer's rank, or a chaplain with a huge chapel in the middle of the building complex or an office in the marketing department of a shopping complex, but the tradition of industrial mission is that negotiating for entry to a new place of work depends on an equal invitation by management and unions.

This freedom of movement is sometimes of great value in the sphere of pastoral care. The bureaucracies of institutions can be short-circuited by a word in the right place at the right time, but it needs to be used with great care as it is easily open to manipulation and can undermine the proper efforts of others to develop good systems of communication.

More often this freedom is described as a springboard for prophetic ministry. Many years ago, working as a chaplain's assistant in an old psychiatric hospital, I felt that some of the practices of the nurses were bordering on the cruel. On one occasion they lined up long-stay patients and kicked footballs at them from close range. I said and did nothing, but the following year my successor was so horrified that, after seeming to get nowhere with the authorities in the hospital, he went to the newspapers about it and it became a front-page story. It may have been the right thing to do but the work of the chaplaincy in that hospital was greatly undermined, so my sense, looking back, is that neither I nor the assistant who followed me got it right.

The prophetic word from the margin and often from right outside is different from the word spoken by someone on the inside. The chaplain, because of having permission to be there, is always an insider. In this case the prophetic word only has a chance of being heard if certain things are in place. First, the level of trust and the quality of relationships needs to be very high. Secondly, the prophet who speaks from the inside needs to demonstrate a real understanding of the organization or institution, its business and its politics. Finally, the prophet needs to decide the way in which the word is spoken, and assess the potential cost of speaking. For the chaplain, called to represent the values of the Kingdom of God, these are not easy decisions to make and the professional skills need to be learned and honed.

A third area of professional skill relates to liturgy. Recently a hospital chaplain conducted a funeral liturgy for the closure of a Victorian building that had been home for many psychiatric patients and the working environment of nurses for over a hundred years. As new buildings sprang up in the grounds to cater for the modern needs of psychiatric care the shadow of the old building held many memories, and a liturgy seemed appropriate and was welcomed by many. There were a few Christians among those who attended and there were many of other faiths and none, yet all were bound together in their desire for a ritual expression of closure and transition. All shared a sense of the spiritual and found their needs contained by the words and actions shaped specially for the occasion by the chaplain.

Three things are combined here: the ability to sense and interpret the needs of people and institutions for ritual expression; a deep grounding in the liturgical expressions of the Christian tradition; and an ability to shape words, music, movement, space and silence in a way that gathers up the hearts and minds of people into the presence of the God who comes to us in Jesus Christ, through Holy Spirit. On almost every occasion the majority of any congregation in such circumstances will be unfamiliar with both the traditional and the modern range of Christian worship practices. So the task is to honour the wisdom of generations of worshippers held and expressed in the traditional, to speak to and on behalf of the specific context and maybe reshape the normal ingredients of liturgy so that they resonate with the spirituality of those whom we rather negatively name as the 'unchurched'. Such liturgies, to be Christian, need to speak to the whole person, call institutions to Kingdom values and point to life in Christ.

Good practice at 'base camp'

In this section I want to look at the balance we need to achieve between our experience of working in the public place, and the reflection on our experience, which needs to be done in the quiet and safety of what I have called 'base camp' with our colleagues, mentors or consultants. The stories that sector ministers tell of their work need to be told, laughed and cried over, struggled with, and prayed about, for they are a potent resource for reflection. These processes offer windows into the changing nature of life in our society, models for ministry and mission, spirituality and theology. For several years I had the privilege of working alongside Margaret Kane,[1] when she was the theological consultant to the North-East, and more recently I have been able to learn from sector ministers working in the diocese of Oxford. This kind of association always seems to raise fascinating questions:

- What is happening to the society in which we live and to its institutions? Are we driven by consumer sensation and if we are how does that relate to the new age spirituality that seems vibrant? Are we losing faith in our institutions, and what are the values that bind us together? What are the implications for the human spirit of new technologies? What does it mean to live in a postmodern multi-faith society?
- What is the gospel for the people among whom we work? How can we find a language of word and action that remains faithful to God, and speaks to the experience of so many people for whom the churches as institutions are flawed beyond redemption, or just irrelevant?
- What theologies sustain our ministry? Do we have a view of taking God into our institutions or do we expect God to be there already, and see our role as one of finding and revealing? What are the differing implications of working with or without the security or burdens of buildings, congregations, rank, or office base? What do we mean when we use 'incarnation' as a model for our ministry?
- What is happening to the person who takes up the role of chaplain, and about the pressures on the shape of that role and on the changing shapes of the system in which that person in role has to work? How marginal is the chaplain, and what kind of power does the freedom to roam really give him?
- How does the chaplain renew himself and in what ways does he belong to the people of God?

There are so many questions that emerge from the experience of this profound and committed engagement with the world beyond the boundaries of the local church, and they challenge not only those who work in them but us all.

Relating to the sending institutions

One of the most popular weekends in our church when I was a child was the missionary weekend. We would have a visit from one or two missionaries who were home on furlough and doing their spell of deputation work. In the days before much television and worldwide travel, few of us had been to the African jungles or the cities of India and it was wonderful to hear about other countries, their culture and religions. We also thanked God for the Christian missionary work (even though we know now that some of it was deeply flawed). These weekends may have been aimed at increasing our giving and recruiting us to be willing to go as missionaries, but they also opened our eyes to issues and concerns that we had never heard of, or had had to think about. The deputation weekend offers us a model for the relationship between sector ministries and the rest of the church which often pays for, authorizes and blesses the work of sector ministry, for it demonstrates that it is as important to relate to the 'sending' church as it is to those who enagage in the sector.

The difficulty is that it often feels like, and often is, the fact that the churches as institutions are dominated by the concerns that arise from the care of local congregations, their ministers and buildings. The 'sending' churches seem to have little interest in sector ministry. We are faced with a dominant and domestic model of what it means to be church – a worshipping community led by an authorized or ordained minister, usually located in a set of buildings which include something we call a church, and relating to other similar worshipping communities based on geography. Although in Anglican ecclesiology the focus of unity is the diocese and its bishop, it is the parish and its well-being that lies at the heart of policy and deployment of resources. This means that sector ministry is small in terms of money and people and peripheral to the interests of parochial church councils and synods.

There was research conducted by the Tavistock Clinic[2] in the 1960s about the difficulties commercial companies had with their sales representatives who on the whole bonded too well with their company's rival representatives in the hotels they all frequented. Moreover, they seemed to be more loyal to the customers they visited regularly than to the companies that hired them to outsell their rivals. There is no doubt that many in sector ministry feel the same – a greater loyalty to their sector and to their colleagues than to the denomination that sponsors them. Indeed there are often debates in Anglican synods about the costs of sector ministry and their irrelevance when weighed against the needs for lower parish contributions and more parish priests. There may be benefits for those in sector ministry from being left alone to pursue their own vision and interest, but there is a great loss to the church as a whole and I think that this is the single most important professional issue to face.

There are a number of ways of framing this. One is to talk about the wisdom and insights of those on the margins. Sector ministry, on the margins of institutional church life, and unencumbered by the concerns of 'parish', can have a perspective which all need to hear. There is something particular to be learned about grace when there is nothing on offer apart from a relationship. A particular parochial minister may not be very good or gracious but there will always be people who want baptisms, weddings and funerals, so there are deals to be struck. The sector minister on the other hand has only a relationship of care to offer and so digs deep into the grace of Christ.[3] This experience needs to be named and shared so that we can all reflect upon its implications in our own ministries.

Another way of looking at this, still from the margin, is to acknowledge that sector ministers often work in sections of society untouched by the normal round of parish life. There are two things of great value here for the churches. The first is to learn about that sector of society from people who are fully involved in it and can reflect about it from a theological perspective. Whether it be agricultural concerns, the prison service, the high-tech industries or the leading edge of genetic research there need to be good feedback systems so that bishops, parish ministers and the people of God can be enriched and informed about the issues that face us all. Secondly, there is a particular theological insight to be gained, and this is because sector ministry offers some kind of laboratory experiment in gospel. In a multicultural society, issues of the enculturation of the gospel have become very important. Local congregational life is on the whole 'encultured' in white, middle-class Englishness, and we have some good knowledge about how to address this sector of society with gospel. But what about the homeless, or those who frequent, not our churches, but our shopping malls on Sundays, or our universities, or those who experience racism as part of their daily life? How is gospel to be encultured in these settings? It is the sector ministers and chaplains who are exploring these issues and from whom we have so much to learn. The lookout on the *Titanic* may not have been at the heart of things and may have been junior but it would have been wise to heed his call!

There is a more general reflection from the margins, for those in sector ministry have much to share with the wider church in shaping the church for the future. An example would be the wealth of experience sector ministers have in chatting with and understanding people who on the whole have little or nothing to do with church. Why are people so interested in spiritual things and so willing to chat with chaplains, but see no need to go to their local church? What are the ways which chaplains have found to speak the name of Christ that makes sense to those who would not even attend an Alpha course or a Seeker Service? How can we find new ways of doing outreach work, and are there strategies for mission and evangelism that are better done away from the local church base (or are Alpha courses and Seeker Services and friendship evangelism the only ways?)? What are the things that interest and concern people?

A second frame is the idea of liminality. This is referred to by Gerald

Arbuckle in the following chapter, and I want to relate it specifically to the work of Kenneth Mason.[4] Here sector ministry (the liminal) holds the energy of anti-structure in the church while the parochial and diocesan hold structure. There is a dynamic and important conflict between structure and anti-structure which refines the old and brings the new to birth. 'The nothingness of the liminal condition, however, is a challenge to everyone and everything to justify its claim to be something. It is a reminder to us all of the nothingness out of which we have been brought [. . .] It is rather that structure *(the parish system)* is followed, shadowed, haunted by anti-structure [. . .] Human beings devise all kinds of ways for getting things done, very necessary and proper to the world's work *(structure)*. Nevertheless, unless these devices are menaced ever so gently with irony or lightened by conviviality *(anti-structure)* they will fail to serve humanity.'[5]

An example might be a debate about the nature of community. The commitment of the church as structure is to the local congregation or parish. Although in earlier times people lived and worked and worshipped in the same locality, today this has almost completely broken down, not only with work and home separated, but with transport, suburbia and global communications. The question of belonging is no longer a foregone conclusion based on geography. I may sleep in a suburb or village, work in a city centre, belong to one or two leisure groups, meet up with old friends on a regular holiday and network with others through a notice board on the Internet. My church, around the corner from my sleeping accommodation, may be the last place to which I, as a Christian, would look for community and an appropriate worship that symbolized the people of God. It may be that in this new diversity of belonging, the holy place (often a mediaeval church building) becomes the magnet for disparate people to gather to construct community, and to all intents and purposes the consumer church is created. It may be that a group of Christians in my workplace is the right centre for my celebration of word and sacrament. Anti-structure needs to challenge the dominant model of the parish church, not because it is out to destroy something that is valuable, but so that clear sight and argued intelligence can be brought to bear on all our priorities.

There are two other key issues engaging the mind of the churches at the moment and sector ministry has much to offer on both of them. The first has to do with the whole question of ministry, public and private, ordained and lay. Take any place of work that has a chaplain – a school, university, factory or shopping centre. There will also be Christian women and men living out their faith at every level of the organization. There may well be someone ordained but carrying on their secular employment. What is distinctive about these vocations and the ways in which ministry can be offered and received? What is distinctive about ordination, if anything? What is the difference between an ordained chaplain and a lay chaplain, since both have the role and authorization? What is the balance between the public ministry of the ordained, if they have declared it, the chaplain, and those lay people who have let it be known that they are committed Christians? What about the private ministry of those who have chosen to say as little as possible about their faith and who may never be known as Christians in their workplace? It may be that these are the questions of the traditional church which is dominated by hierarchy, order and authorization and the world of sector ministry needs to prick the balloon of self-importance by showing how irrelevant it all is. But if these questions have any mileage then the experience of sector ministry has great value.

The second key issue has to do with questions of ecumenism and interfaith. On the whole the major denominations are still locked up in their structures of power and their buildings and congregations are cheek by jowl in towns and cities. Even in new housing areas where ecumenical co-operation has allowed shared buildings and Local Ecumenical Partnerships, the heavy weight of sponsoring bodies and denominational expectations drags down vision and experiment. In some sectors, of course, these patterns of division and control remain, but in others there is the glorious freedom to experiment, and some of the stories in this book bear testimony to the creative possibilities. The spectre of interfaith chapels and worship, and interfaith chaplaincy teams worries and disturbs the churches, but unless we experiment we can never be clear about where the boundaries to such co-operation should be.

This is not just an internal question about organization and co-operation for it taps into the key questions of the spirituality of the many different cultures that make up modern society in the muck of the world. The huge success of the film *Titanic* and the extraordinary events surrounding the death of Diana, Princess of Wales, open up issues about the unconscious archetypes and myths that speak to us women and men whatever our conscious faith and religious affiliation, and address our longings, our hopes and our fears. This undoubtedly is the language of our spirit, and sector ministry, so close to many religions and none, has the potential of offering leadership to the church in this area.

I have offered all these as examples of the way in which there needs to be a more vigorous engagement between the institutional churches and the world of sector ministry. I started this section with the model of a missionary deputation and used a story from research done about sales representatives, but there may be a more obvious metaphor for the relationship between sector ministry and the rest of the church. Is sector ministry more like a research and development group in a company? Research and development is often the first to go when finances are short, but is the part of the company which holds the creative edge, but only if it can stay in close touch with the rest of the organization.

Notes

1 M. Kane, *Gospel in Industrial Society* (London: SCM, 1980) and *What Kind of God?: Reflections on Working with People and Churches in North East England* (London, SCM, 1986).

2 E. J. Miller and A. K. Rice, *Systems of Organisation* (London: Tavistock, 1967).

3 W. H. Vanstone, *Farewell in Christ* (London: Darton, Longman and Todd, 1997), see ch. 4.

4 K. Mason, *Priesthood and Society* (Norwich: Canterbury Press, 1992).

5 Ibid., p. 69.

17

Chaplaincy, teams and ecumenism

Gerald Arbuckle

'Cease to dwell on days gone by and to brood over past history. Here and now I will do a new thing; this moment it will break from the bud. Can you not perceive it?' (lsaiah 43:18–19).

Ministry has as its primary task the development of 'a community with an alternative, liberated imagination that has the courage and the freedom to act in a different vision and a different perception of reality'.[1] Chaplains, like all pastors, must be committed to this task.

Leadership, refounding and team effort

Where what has to be done is uncertain or ill-focused, as in times of rapid change or chaos in which considerable innovative skills are required, a transforming style of leadership is necessary – one based on trust and mutuality. The task of transforming leadership is primarily to foster a collaborative or team atmosphere in which this trust and mutuality exist as prerequisites for creative action or strategies for change.

The process of refounding is an exercise of transforming leadership involving three categories of people: *authority position people, refounding people,* and *renewal people.*[2]

Authority position people

'Authority position people' have by their appointment official power to stop or foster change; they are a group's official gatekeepers to change (for example bishops, synods). Their primary task is to create a proactive organizational atmosphere, or culture, that is continually expanding its capacity for pastoral creativity and encouraging innovative people to act for the common good. Authentic authority position people recognize this truth and keep calling their organizations to own their own chaos, to abandon the irrelevant and to be open to the vision of the radically new. They accept the fact that innovation is a messy process. It involves the personalities, emotions and pecularities of many inventive people. Pastoral creativity, like all innovation, does not always work neatly. In-depth culture change is slow and involves much darkness, trial and error, and evaluation.

Refounding people

A refounding person understands the purpose for which the organization was founded, and creatively finds new ways to organize in changed circumstances. 'Refounding people', with their above-average gifts of imagination, intuition, innovation, collaboration, courage and hope, are dreamers who do, contemplatives who act. They are able to return to the founding experience of an organization and, in a collaborative way, take quantum leap creative action that responds to the causes of contemporary pastoral problems. Passionately committed to the vision of refounding, they are not lightly dissuaded from action. The people who invented the personal computer made such a quantum leap in theory and action, as did the people who invented the very popular Post-It Notes at 3M company in the early 1970s. History shows that refounding people are rarely easy to be with, simply because they challenge our comfortable status quo. The reality is that any organization that domesticates its rebels has won its peace but has lost its future.

The churches urgently and continuously need pastoral rebels who, refusing to be domesticated by the forces of tradition, challenge false ecclesiastical peace and denial. Here are two examples of refounding. In the pastoral care of the dying, Dame Cicely Saunders is a refounder of the hospice care movement. Saunders came to see that palliative care exists not only to affirm life and individuality, but also, in the words of St Christopher's Hospice Mission Statement, 'to help patients with strong and unfamiliar emotions, to assist them to explore meaning, purpose, and value in their lives. To offer opportunity to reconcile and heal relationships and complete important personal tasks.'[3] Saunders's approach has dramatically influenced pastoral care today in many Western countries. Dr Christiane Brusselmans, the designer of what is generally known as the Adult Catechumenate and to Roman Catholics as the Rite of Christian Initiation of Adults (RCIA) after Vatican II, created a refounding or transforming vision for evangelizers that recognized the need for people seeking baptism to move slowly and by recognized stages through the conversion process with and into the ecclesial community.[4]

Renewal people

The third category of collaborators in refounding are 'renewal people'. They lack the outstanding gifts of refounders, but with their 'nuts-and-bolts' skills and willing commitment to the group's mission, they are indispensable collaborators in the refounding process.

Refounding people as 'dissenters' in the church

Refounding people in the church today are those:

— who have gifts to grasp the *communitarian* and prophetic vision of the gospel message;
— who can imaginatively relate it in pastorally creative ways to the dramatically new needs of today's world by going to the very roots of these issues;
— who draw others, through conversion and commitment to the vision, into a believing, worshipping and evangelizing community.

Jesus Christ as a model for refounding

Jesus is the model of what to expect in refounding people. Jesus emphasized in word and action the importance of team building both as a way to evangelize and as a model of the fullness of the kingdom to come: 'And he appointed twelve; they were to be his companions' (Mark 3:14–15); 'May they be one . . . so that the world may believe it was you who sent me' (John 17:21). Jesus repeatedly and creatively uses his imagination in teaching, for example, in his use of parables, and his vivid description of nature and human experiences (Luke 6:39). There is remarkable adaptability in his involvement in highly technical arguments with prominent scholars of his day (Luke 20:19–44) or in his preaching to ordinary people in ways they could readily understand (Mark 12:37). He repeatedly goes to the roots of the problems of his day:

— by attacking the racism of his day (Luke 10:29–37);
— by breaking down the gender barriers through conversing with women on the basis of equality (John 4:7ff., 27);
— by bridging the social barriers through associating with tax collectors (Luke 15:1–3);
— by confronting the ideological barriers in his conversations with the Pharisees (Luke 7:44).[5]

Like the prophets before him Jesus has the gift of mourning; he recognizes there must be death before there is life: 'As he drew near and came in sight of the city, he shed tears over it . . . "(They) will leave not one stone standing on another within you, because you did not recognise the moment of your visitation"' (Luke 19:41, 44). Like all authentic founding and refounding people Jesus has a sense of humour. He does not take himself too seriously, but trusts in the power of the Father. He, the King of kings, is born in a stable, and dies on the cross! Nothing could be more incongruous – a life of 'divine incongruity'! Yet nothing could be more powerful in conveying the truth of his words: 'I have come so that they may have life and have it to the full' (John 10:10). And the source of Christ's humour? His detachment from self, his humility: 'His state was divine, yet he did not cling to his equality with God but emptied himself to assume the condition of a slave' (Philippians 2:6–7).

To pray is to acknowledge the suffering and misery of the world within oneself and without. Christ does just that to his Father, giving refounders of his mission to the contemporary world a critical lesson: 'In his anguish he prayed even more earnestly, and his sweat fell to the ground like great drops of blood' (Luke 22:44). Prayer is also a listening to the Father, a being with him; this Jesus does, as a necessary part of the rhythm of his life as the founder of our faith (Luke 9:28–36). So also chaplains who are called to refound their ministries. Without personal prayer, and shared prayer with their fellow team workers, they can never maintain their commitment to a radical restructuring of their ministries.

Refounding in action: practical hints for chaplains

Team work
Refounding cannot take place without team work; there must be a strong and positive interaction between people at all levels of ministry and particularly between authority position, refounding and renewal people. If there is to be the development of a faith community with an alternative pastoral, liberated imagination people involved in catalysing the refounding process must themselves model this community in their relationships together. But teams of chaplains within the same denomination or across denominational lines do not emerge, nor are they sustained, easily.

Team work is the result of a high level of *interdependency*; that is, each person in the team has his/her role clarified and feels responsible for, and is supported in, its achievement, but works to combine his/her actions with those of others in view of a commonly accepted vision and mission. The stress is on *interdependency*, not dependency or counter-dependency. Jon Katzenbach and Douglas Smith define the difference between groups and teams: 'Groups become teams through *disciplined action*. They *shape* a common purpose, *agree* on performance goals, *define* a common working approach, *develop* high levels of complementary *skills*, and *hold* themselves mutually accountable for results. And, as with any effective discipline, they never stop doing any of these things.'[6] Authority position, refounding and renewal people must all be clear about the primary purpose of working together, namely to build faith-based communities that challenge according to gospel values a secularized society around them. Once they effectively commit themselves to this vision, then they begin to move from being a group of individuals to a team for mission.

Role of authority position people

Authority position people, that is bishops or pastoral directors, first need to know their role in refounding and keep to it. There are three functions to their role: they need to find pastorally creative chaplains, place them in ways that they can be most effective and protect them from undue interference from outsiders. The positioning of creative people, especially refounding people, is a critical and controversial issue. The enormity of the challenge is best understood by describing the seductive power of the *cultural* status quo.

Sociologist Peter Berger defines culture as *nomos* (order) because it protects us from the awesome insecurities of chaos (*anomy*). *Nomos* is 'an area of meaning carved out of a vast mass of meaninglessness, a small clearing of lucidity in a formless, dark, almost ominous jungle'.[7] When a personal or group culture dramatically disintegrates or is threatening to do so, people experience the darkness of meaninglessness, a crushing taste of chaos, as for example happens at the sudden death of a dear friend. The postmodern world in which we live is itself in ever increasing change and fragmentation and people suffer this fear-evoking chaos with all its terrors at various levels of their daily life as never before.

Though experiences of chaos, e.g. the loss of a job, or the breakdown of traditional values and structures, can be confusing, even terrifying, paradoxically contact with chaos or the world of the unpredictable or unknown is critical *if* there is to be creativity in life or culture. Innovative scientists, poets, philosophers, artists, creative chaplains, refounding people, all have one thing in common: they venture into the unknown, into the unpredictable, into chaos, in search of new meanings or new ways of doing things.

We can be ambivalent toward these people. On the one hand, we can appreciate them for offering us through their initiatives and inventions better ways of living. On the other hand, especially until we have become used to the interesting things they provide us with, we *fear* them simply because they venture into the unknown world, the world of disorder and insecurity, the chaos of non-meaning. Berger expresses our fear of the innovator in this way: 'the individual who strays seriously from the socially defined programs can be considered not only a fool or a knave but a madman.'[8] For this reason it is 'natural' for people to want to marginalize, de-energize or excessively control the innovator because of his/her ways that disturb the comforting security of the culturally predictable.

To prevent these negative reactions from destroying or weakening the creative gifts of pastoral innovators it is necessary to set up structures to protect them, for example, the establishment by authority position people of clear and simple lines of accountability so that creative people are not trapped in unnecessary, de-energizing defence of their work.

Jesus himself was quite literally commenting on the seductive and crushing power of groups caught up in the chaos when he said: 'No one puts a piece of unshrunken cloth onto an old cloak, because the patch pulls away from the cloak and the tear gets worse. Nor do people put new wine into old wineskins; otherwise, the skins burst, the wine runs out, and the skins are lost. No; they put new wine in fresh skins and both are preserved' (Matthew 9:16–17). Each effort at refounding requires some degree of protection lest it be smothered by the existing structures and attitudes of the surrounding institutions or pastoral organizations.

In brief, the biblically based pastoral wisdom is: build new structures and foster simple, clean lines of accountability for ongoing evaluation in order to allow space for renewal and refounding people to function freely and constructively. I call this guideline: 'the new belongs elsewhere.'[9] Do not expect creative people to do the impossible – namely, to convert structures and people who stubbornly resist change because of their fears of the unpredictable. Recall the instruction of Jesus to the apostles: 'And if anyone does not welcome you or listen to what you have to say, as you walk out of the house or town shake the dust from your feet' (Matthew 10:14). If people are not interested in refounding, even more so if they seek to subvert the process deliberately or otherwise, then following Jesus' advice our energies must be unequivocally directed elsewhere. Go wherever there is life, not death: 'Leave the dead to bury their dead; your duty is to go and spread the news of the kingdom of God' (Luke 9:60).

Authority position people need courage to protect innovative chaplains from undue outside interference. They need to be aware that refounding will inevitably be disruptive. No matter what care they use there will be people and organizations that will continue to feel lost and unhappy with the changes, strongly condemning those who dare to disrupt the status quo or support those who do so. Ultimately it is the mission of Jesus Christ that has the priority of rights, not irrelevant pastoral structures or processes.

Chaplains as liminal people
In any significant change either at the personal or group level there is the stage which is called *liminality*,[10] that is, a 'betwixt and between' phase in which social statuses and roles that are important in daily living are temporarily suspended and people interact at the level of 'raw humanity'. An experience of 'pure' brotherhood/sisterhood relations (technically called *communitas*) resulting from this interaction can provide an enduring bond that can persist beyond the experience. Another word for liminality is *chaos*; at least

temporarily the supportive structures of everyday life are suspended or are seen as no longer important for personal identity or self-esteem. For example, people finding themselves in a lifeboat fighting to survive in tumultuous seas rapidly forget their widely different social statuses/roles in society. It is as though they have been reduced or ground down to a uniform common condition to be fashioned anew and endowed with additional powers to enable them to cope with whatever lies ahead. For evermore they can relate to one another at a level of unity that outsiders can rarely understand.

In summary, liminality is an intrinsically unstable and uncertain condition, involving the embracing of social meaninglessness (*anomy*), or chaos, for the sake of the expanded creative possibilities it can provide. There is no certainty whatsover that people will survive a liminal experience; they may struggle nostalgically to seek the supportive refuge of their former social statuses or they may become paralysed by the forces of the chaos itself. People in their right mind do not 'stand on their social or status dignity' in a lifeboat when faced with the threat of death. If they are to survive they will immediately and energetically collaborate in order to survive. In a true sense liminality can be an initiation into 'real living', that is a stage when people must confront fundamental questions about what is or is not important in life.

People in a liminality stage of life's journey may be termed *liminars*. Chaplains are *liminars* or 'people on the margins', 'betwixt-and-between people'. Chaplains are *liminars*, firstly because they are not pastorally involved in 'ordinary' ministry, that is in territorially based parochial services. Secondly, they are often pastorally concerned for people who are themselves socially, politically or economically on the margins, e.g. the homeless, prisoners, sick, the dying, seafarers, police. Thirdly, in a world of economic rationalism that has revitalized the cult of individualism and patriarchical managerialism, teamwork is considered unbecoming to an authentic postmodernist. Teamwork is seen as a sign of weakness. Fourthly, since teamwork is not usual in 'normal pastoral' activities, chaplains are considered 'outside the normal', a little suspect by traditional ministers. Fifthly, when chaplains commit themselves to *ecumenical* teamwork they may further isolate themselves from the mainstream ministers, who might uphold rigid denominational boundaries. Sixthly, chaplains often have to minister in highly secularized environments where they are seen as irrelevant, e.g. in public hospitals chaplains increasingly have to defend themselves before medical authorities to prove that their ministry is important for the healing of patients.[11]

Chaplains, as pastoral *liminars*, must consequently expect to be little understood by people of other ministries and not infrequently subtly or not-so-subtly marginalized. For example, expressions like the following can be directed against them: 'These chaplains think they are special, but when they have to work as hard as we do in the parishes then they will truly know what work is!' The ministry of chaplains can be an intensely lonely one, simply because it is liminal or outside the 'normal' pastoral services.

Yet, at the same time liminality offers people *the* opportunity to return to what is essential in the founding story of our faith and from that inner journey there can come an energy beyond all human imagination. This was surely the case *par excellence* with the Israelites. Despite their many faults they discovered, in the chaos of their initiation into the promised land and withdrawal from the securities of Egypt, that Yahweh remained creatively faithful and protective even though he/she seemed at times to be distant and uninterested in them: 'you of all the nations shall be my very own for all the earth is mine' (Exodus 19:5). The memory of this exodus chaos and the abiding presence of Yahweh would be for the Israelites at the time of any future chaos, e.g. the exile, a dramatic source of energy to keep going: life can emerge out of the most traumatic experience of chaos. If chaplains own their powerlessness there is nothing they creatively cannot do pastorally *together*; bonded together on the pastoral margins they can courageously challenge traditional ecclesiastical and pastoral structures. They can be in the forefront of refounding the church in a secularizing age! Alone they cannot survive and be ministerially effective.

Let me go further into this insight. Chaplains are called to refound ministry, that is, to go to the margins of chaos in order to reach pastorally the heart of contemporary problems, e.g. in prisons, in psychiatric hospitals. This is an impossible task if they are not first struggling to enter into their own personal chaos. It is there that they discover their own sinfulness, fears and prejudices, and thus their own desperate need in hope of God's ever-healing presence. As St Paul writes succinctly: 'I am most happy, then, to be proud of my weaknesses, in order to feel the protection of Christ's power over me . . . For when I am weak, then I am strong' (2 Corinthians 12:9–10). Sensitive to their own helplessness without Christ, they experience an empathy with the afflicted around them and a hope and trust in the all-loving and forgiving Jesus.

Recall a significant comment by Mark the evangelist when reflecting on the failure of the three disciples to support Jesus in his intense liminal loneliness in the garden of Gethsemane: They did not know how to help him, because 'they did not know what to say to him' (Mark 14:40). They did not know how to help or what to say, because they had not yet admitted to their own inner chaos, powerlessness and fragility. Without having made this inner journey, they could feel no empathy or compassion with Jesus in his suffering.

The example of Esther, a liminal person, may also guide chaplains confronted with the tensions of the liminality of their ministry. Esther is aware that the Israelites are in danger of being annihilated and that something must be done to stop this; Yahweh in his providence must intervene and Esther is filled with fear that she must be the agent of God's intervention. She becomes compassionate and pastorally creative simply because she is ever conscious of the chaos within and without and her own consequent desperate need for Yahweh's help. From this inner journey there comes a divine strength to act:

> My Lord, our King, the Holy One,
> come to my help, for I am alone
> and have no helper but you
> and am about to take my life in my hands. (Esther 14:3–4)

Esther, in her chaos, returns to the founding experience of Israel and of Yahweh's abiding love. From this reowning of the founding story Esther is strengthened to creative action for her people:

> I have been taught from infancy
> . . . that you, Lord, have chosen
> Israel out of all the nation . . .
> Never let our ruin be a matter for laughter . . .
> Remember, Lord; reveal yourself in the time of
> distress . . .
> O God, whose strength prevails over all,
> listen to the voice of the desperate,
> save us from the hand of the wicked,
> and free me from my fear!' (Esther 14:5, 11–12, 19)

Chaplains as ritual leaders of grief[12]
The churches and their ministers today are experiencing an overload of grief. Church attendance in the Western world is dropping at a steady rate; Christians are confused, even in chaos, as they hear of the alarming reports of ecological disasters, from deforestation in Brazil and Indonesia to the 'greenhouse effect' and acid rain. Add AIDS and the chronic poverty and oppression in the Third World, and the irrelevance with which people view the teachings of Jesus Christ, and it is not hard to see why apocalyptic visions, with their calls of impending doom, are currently fashionable.[13]

Reactions to these apostolic challenges differ among Christians. There are many symptoms of grieving: anger, sadness, denial and avoidance of the loss of the familiar. Some of us nostalgically gather together to restore apostolic methods and liturgical practices of old, which are totally out of touch with Christ's call to evangelize the world as it is today. Others retreat into a private or sect-like fundamentalist religion which refuses any involvement with the mission of Christ to the world.

Chaplains, in their role as prophetic liminal or refounding leaders in chaos, must *inter alia* be grief leaders, calling fellow Christians and churches to let go the familiar and historically irrelevant in order to risk the unknown. We Westerners, however, have culturally lost the art of dying, so we must build appropriate rituals of loss, that the new and creative may enter into our lives and communities. Mourning experiences of traditional cultures, including the cultures of the Old and New Testaments, can guide us.

In a traditional culture, the community's leaders exercise a pivotal role in challenging the culture to recognize loss and the dangers of chronic denial in all its devious forms. After the ascension of Jesus, his disciples were in grave danger of denying the fact that he was no longer with them. Their loss and denial had to be openly articulated and dealt with; otherwise, they would not welcome the dramatic, transforming newness of the Spirit. Luke describes the role of the two angels as ritual community leaders: the disciples 'were still gazing up into the heavens when two men dressed in white stood beside them. "Men of Galilee, why do you stand here looking up at the skies?"' (Acts 1:10–11). Jesus was disengaging himself from his followers and achieving a new status beside the Father. The disciples were encouraged to move to the next stage of their grieving process. They left for an upper room in Jerusalem – their liminality experience – in order to pray over and to ponder the loss as well as the vision of the promised, fear-creating newness yet to come at Pentecost: 'Together they devoted themselves to constant prayer' (Acts 1:14).

At Emmaus, Jesus himself is the ritual leader, challenging the two disciples to acknowledge their loss in a creative way. Jesus leads them through the first stage of separation from their 'normal' life, in which they freely express their anger and sadness that things have not turned out as they had so sincerely hoped. Jesus does not judge or condemn their anger (Luke 24:17–24). They then enter the liminality phase of their journey; here Jesus, having obtained their trust, strongly challenges them to recognize their loss, accept it and move on. Then they will be open to a community and personal newness beyond human imagination as a result of Jesus's death and resurrection (Luke 24:25–32).

Jesus, and the prophets before him, and Moses model for chaplains the role and qualities of grief leadership within their faith communities. They are to be future-oriented or hope-filled people, since they believe their primary task is to challenge ecclesiastical and secular cultures to interiorize a vision not yet realized. They recognize when people and groups are locked into unconscious denial of loss; they believe they must publicly articulate this refusal to face uncomfortable realities, even though the process of confrontation may isolate them as leaders. Their task, difficult though it is, is to empower the group to assume responsibility for its own mourning.

The temptation to allow the group to become over dependent on the grief leader must be resisted at all costs. Neither Moses nor Jesus succumbed to this temptation. As the Israelites are about to enter the promised land Moses slips away, in a spirit of remarkable patience and detachment, to die alone on a mountain and to rest in an unmarked grave (Deuteronomy 34:1–7). When the two disciples at Emmaus are in danger of becoming overdependent on Jesus' presence, he withdraws to allow them to test their new-found apostolic strength by returning to Jerusalem (Luke 24:30–35).

Conclusion

The gospel message is highly subversive when people refuse to tolerate individualism and pastoral mediocrity. Chaplains are *liminal* people, that is they do not belong to the mainstream or traditional ministries of the churches and this places them in a powerful, liberating position to be evangelically subversive. At the same time it renders them vulnerable, like all prophets, to being misunderstood, even marginalized for their pastorally dissident words and behaviour.

Their experience on the margins can be the catalyst for enormous pastoral creativity, provided they act together in support of one another. With teamwork, and backed by people in authority, they can use their vulnerability to develop not only radical creative responses to the pastoral needs of the people they serve, but also to challenge the wider Christian community to break attachments to irrelevant methods and structures of evangelization, including unnecessary denominational barriers, for the sake of the mission of Jesus Christ.

Notes

1   W. Brueggemann, *Hopeful Imagination; Prophetic Voices in Exile* (Philadelphia: Fortress Press, 1986), p. 99.
2   See G. A. Arbuckle, *Refounding the Church: Dissent for Leadership* (London: Geoffrey Chapman/Maryknoll, NY: Orbis Books, 1993), pp. 98–127.
3   C. Saunders, 'Hospices worldwide: a mission statement' in C. Saunders and R. Kastenbaum (eds), *Hospice Care on the International Scene* (New York: Springer, 1997), p. 6.
4   See G. A. Arbuckle, *Refounding the Church*, p. 103.
5   See G. A. Arbuckle, *Earthing the Gospel: An Inculturation Handbook for Pastoral Workers* (London: Geoffrey Chapman/Maryknoll, NY: Orbis Books, 1990), pp. 214–17.
6   J. R. Katzenbach and D. K. Smith, *The Wisdom of Teams* (New York: Harper Business, 1993), pp. 14–15.
7   P. Berger, *The Sacred Canopy: Elements of a Sociological Theory of Religion* (New York: Doubleday, 1969), p. 23. For a commentary on Berger's definitions see G. A. Arbuckle, *Out of Chaos: Refounding Religious Congregations* (Mahwah: NY: Paulist Press/London: Geoffrey Chapman, 1988), pp. 14–17, 47–9.
8   P. Berger, *Sacred Canopy*, p. 24.
9   See G. A. Arbuckle, *Refounding the Church*, pp. 119–20, 149.
10 See V. Turner, *The Ritual Process: Structures and Anti-Structure* (Ithaca, NY: Cornell University Press, 1967), pp. 94–203 and *passim*.

11 See L. Carey *et al.*, 'Health policy and well-being: hospital chaplaincy' in H. Gardner (ed.), *Health Policy in Australia* (Melbourne: Oxford University Press, 1997), pp. 190–210.

12 See G. A. Arbuckle, *From Chaos to Mission: The Refounding of Religious Life Formation* (London: Geoffrey Chapman/Collegeville, MN: Liturgical Press, 1993), pp. 187–207.

13 For a relevant overview of the pastoral challenges confronting the churches see I. Osborn, *Restoring the Vision: The Gospel and Modern Culture* (London: Mowbray, 1995).

18

Where is God in all this? Exploring and affirming those in sector ministry

James Woodward

Introduction

Part of the agenda behind the production of this book concerned the misunderstandings and perhaps prejudices linked with those in sector ministry. On a personal note I have experienced these misunderstandings during the course of my own ministry over the past decade. Some disappointment was expressed when I took up the job of chaplain to the Bishop of Oxford in 1987. This disappointment reflected mild ambivalence about church management and bureaucracy. Was it an appropriate use of a priest to assist a diocesan bishop in his administrative work? Driving, carrying suitcases and answering the telephone seemed to be incompatible for some with the language of vocation! When in 1990 I decided to seek employment in the National Health Service as a chaplain the expression of bemusement was even sharper. 'Don't you feel up to working in a parish?' was the way a pompous archdeacon expressed his own lack of sympathy with health-care chaplaincy. I often felt that my development and training as a Bishop's Chaplain in administration, conflict management and seeing the diocese as an organization, with all its strengths and weaknesses, was first-rate preparation for the challenges of the National Health Service. When I eventually decided to respond positively to an opportunity to be a parish priest and complete my research and writing, the response of some was to greet me back into the *mainstream* church, as if my sector experience had been part of some misspent youth. By chance as I reflect on the earlier chapters of this book I am preparing to move once again.

The move takes me into a unique in-between world as parish priest and Master of the Lady Katherine Leveson Hospital. In this post I shall be licensed by the bishop but work under a group of governors for a secular institution with its roots firmly in a Christian vision.

This personal note is necessary by way of explaining some of my own biases and presuppositions. I share the editor's belief that sector ministry is both misunderstood and undervalued by the church. However, having worked in a number of contexts, the divisions and assumptions both amongst sector ministers and parochial clergy demand further interrogation and a more subtle and coherent representation. The reflections that follow are therefore inevitably limited, partial and deliberately open-ended.

Faithful presence – ministry or mission?

The overwhelming impression that emerges from reading the reflections of individuals and groups working within particular sectors is that of a persistent, faithful presence in a very wide diversity of situations. Here the minister encounters a huge spectrum of people in their own particular contexts with a rich tapestry of hopes, needs and agendas, in spite of the continued steady decline of organized religion. Within the chapters of this book we see a startling measure of energy, persistence and creativity in ministry. Preconceptions about the church, God and clergy are broken down. Lives are changed through sensitive and careful listening. Some of the deepest and most profound crises of life are interpreted and healed through a compassionate *being there*. Further, in these difficult and testing situations where women and men have to earn respect through the quality of their relationships there is enormous creativity. Those who have power to change and direct the shape of communities are challenged to think about the spiritual and religious dimension of their choices. Artists are enabled to help us dig deeper into the mystery of our human lives through the support of sector ministry. Business people and industrialists know that there are people who appreciate some of the complex ethical dilemmas facing them in their work. Boys and girls have access to a style of religious nurture which supports and encourages them in their educational adventure. Those who work at sea are given the practical support they need to alleviate isolation. Police, farmers, those who work in the forces, nurses, doctors, academics, shop workers, managers, pilots and air crew all have access to someone who is ready to meet them on their terms and offer appropriate and human support. We can but marvel at the thought of the sheer colour and depth and extensiveness of this sector ministerial work. Countless lives are changed in a multiplicity of ordinary and extraordinary ways.

In this sense we all have much to learn from one another about the nature of ministry and the shape of the church's mission. This process of learning is not facilitated through the sharp divisions set down by those in both parish and sector work. There is a mistaken presupposition running through many of the essays here that the parish or congregation is somehow a more stable entity with the role of the priest or ministry accepted, clear and unambiguous. This does not reflect my experience in Middleton and Wishaw, two small rural parishes in north Warwickshire. While there may be some hangover from a period of stability where churchgoing was more widely part of the weekly round, assumptions and the context have radically changed. Rural parishes are no longer places of long-term stability, but mixed communities where families come and go with some groups commuting long distances to work. There is economic diversity which gives rise to communal tensions and conflicts. The village pub is run by a national brewery along strict centralized guidelines with only nominal interest in the village community. The school has gone and been taken over by a private nursery serving the needs of families from as wide a radius as ten miles away. In a comfortable community where financial security protects most from certain vulnerabilities, there is no more need for religion and the church than there might be in the army barracks, the shopping centre or the airport. Sunday worship has to compete with Tamworth Snow Dome or horse riding. More often it is the only day when parents and children can have a long lie-in in bed and not have to bother to get up and expose themselves to what can often feel alien and irrelevant worship.

In other words, long gone are the days (familiar to me in my first curacy in 1985) when ministry was about being around in a parish, conducting Occasional Offices with care, visiting the sick and depending upon a reasonable number of families to turn up for worship to keep the church both alive and solvent. At one level all ministry, whether from parish or sector, is mission. Mission is no longer the sole prerogative of a section of the church, usually evangelical, who are into that kind of thing. Mission is a prerequisite of all in ministry because of the steady decline of church life and the marginalization of the spiritual and religious dimension. It may be the case then, that those working in parishes understand the consequences of being on the margins as insightfully as those sector clergy in this book. In this sense the division between parish and sector needs to be discarded. There is much learning to be done together as experiences in ministry are attended to with care and are mission-enlivened through prayer, questioning and digging ever deeper into the mystery of working for the Kingdom of God.

What kind of God?

The critical factor in both the preparedness and ability of ministers to continue to learn to grow is space. Individuals and groups need to have space to think, to feel and to reflect. Part of the *activity* of all ministry, motivated perhaps by both a sense of marginalization and defensiveness about the legitimacy of the role, can lead ministry into an intellectual poverty. This particular attitude found expression recently at a clergy meeting when a neighbouring priest, on discovering me reading a book, exclaimed 'Why are you reading those words when there's all those souls in your parish to be saved?' Ministry, from one perspective, is about doing rather than being and thinking. This has significant dangers and this is reflected in the contributions. Understandably the quality of reflection varies and I suspect that this quality is partly dependent upon the investment by each individual minister in time and space to ask questions and explore experience. Put alternatively by using a cooking analogy – too much contemporary thinking is done on the cooker top or in the microwave rather than being carefully marinaded and cooked in the oven. The quality of reflection finds expression in the theological vision which shapes the way we both think and act.

All of us have our own unique stories to tell about how God has got hold of us. We have all asked, and should continue to ask 'What does God want of me?' The combination of our personalities, experiences and contexts leaves us with a variety of understandings of God. These perceptions, or our models of God, can and do give rise to all kinds of patterns of belief. Despite, or perhaps because of, our theological education there is a curious lack of awareness and articulation of the sheer variety of models of God and patterns of belief inside and outside the churches. This silence or absence is evident in these contributions. There is curiously little talk about God. There is a need to share the variety of conceptions of God and to be explicit in exploring both the patterns of belief and models of pastoral practice that follow from them. Theology from this perspective should be rescued from the academy and, rather, ministerial experience be viewed as a resource for education and discovery, where honesty is promoted as points of disagreement and where creativity and imagination are engendered in sharing vision and hope. Ministry needs to be enabled to recover a deeper sense of confidence about God in particular and theological reflection in general. It is interesting to note that many of the contributors chose not to be explicit about their own theological agendas, and with a few notable exceptions, failed to articulate any theological depth in their reflection upon their work.

It would be an interesting exercise to ask the contributors to articulate the main sources of influence on their ministry. It is true that ministers often have little time or commitment to maintaining any interest in theology. Those who

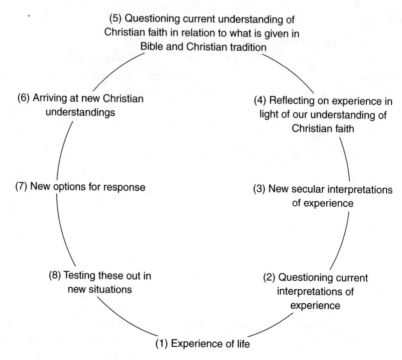

(5) Questioning current understanding of Christian faith in relation to what is given in Bible and Christian tradition

(6) Arriving at new Christian understandings

(4) Reflecting on experience in light of our understanding of Christian faith

(7) New options for response

(3) New secular interpretations of experience

(8) Testing these out in new situations

(2) Questioning current interpretations of experience

(1) Experience of life

Based on a diagram in Margaret Kane, *What Kind of God?* (London: SCM, 1986).

teach theology must be held to account in some respects. Pastoral theology, as a distinct discipline, has in some respects lost its direction. Little innovative, integrated and interdisciplinary thinking is being pursued, and the question remains about whether or not pastoral theology has a distinctive methodology and content. Most of the pastoral theology available to Anglican theological students is largely shaped and influenced by psychology and psycho–therapeutic disciplines. Those responsible for theological nurture and formation in ministry, need to look seriously at these contributions and ask about models of training in the light of this shared experience. Are individuals enabled to make connections and respond creatively by being empowered by their theological education?

The issue of theological reflection has, of course, to do partly with time, but also with a basic attitude that understands that this thinking can make any difference to practice. Margaret Kane provides a useful diagram outlining the process and stages of theological reflection.[1] Is it a process that can enable Christians working in these secular contexts to make sense of their faith in the light of their working experience?

It was interesting to note the different ways in which criticism surfaced within each sector. The school chaplain acknowledges the problems surrounding compulsory worship. Issues around consumerism and Sunday trading were commented on less sharply than might have been the case in an outsider's account. The point that connects us all is a society whose values have changed and are changing, which poses particular threats and opportunities for religion. The armed forces and hospital chaplains have some difficulty in working for institutions which may fundamentally challenge some theological and ethical positions. When did the prison or police chaplain last challenge their own cultures or institutions? Both agree that this is part of the role but it is left as a theoretical position rather than a practical piece of pastoral response. All this may be a reflection of sector ministers working in environments where there is a greater level of control than parish clergy usually experience. It might reflect an anxiety that clergy might not be allowed to control the content of the work. There are profound dangers in the desire to be professional and in the process of professionalization. The freedom from the church which sector ministry may offer is often had at the expense of a critical distance which can speak the truth in love and maintain a creative distance from the changing and sometimes oppressive institutions of society. We need to guard against the picture of God as the great controller, the Colonel-in-Chief, the air traffic controller, the captain of the ship, the headmaster, the prison governor or the Chief Constable! There is a danger in building structures and organizing implicit patterns of belief to reflect this kind of God in our desire for secure professionalism.

Of course we are inheritors of a long and complicated history of the relationship of our faith to culture. In our present social setting we need to take a positive view of secularity because it is within the particular institutions that sector ministers have to work out their Christian obedience to the gospel, making all kinds of acts of faith in the transforming power of Christ.

There is a theological basis for going *with* the culture. There is a need to state a belief in God who is not confined to the religious sphere or embattled against the non-Christian structures. This is a belief in God as involved in all parts of his creation; an incarnational frame of belief rather than a redemptive one through conflict.

Is all authority good?

One of the areas which I perceive as a major theological crisis is in the critique of this new culture as it approaches the end of the millennium, within which the church has to negotiate its place and role.

As mentioned above, sector ministers seem reluctant to take on the role of saboteur, mole or whistle-blower. In what way are these individuals free to work in the way that they feel they should? If God is the headmaster or Chief constable, then is all authority good? There is a need to question the assumption of the implicit goodness of the organization and culture and to ask ourselves how institutionalized we have become. Put another way; do we tell people what they want to hear? With whom, or to whom do we need to belong?

There are barbaric and wicked aspects of all of the institutions within which sector ministers work as well as in the Church. There is tendency within the Health Service to treat healing and health care as commodities whose provision is to be treated as a business in the market. Prisons rarely rehabilitate individuals and seem only, at times, to serve the purposes of making society feel at ease and safe. Many schools may be committed to teaching but know little about the education of the whole person. We are trapped in an economic system within which commercialism and the spirituality of retail therapy is all pervading. This originates, in part, from the temporary eclipse of the idea and ideal of a caring society. Is it true that today altruism has become a private hobby? Has the publicly accepted moral assumption that resources should be used for the common good been eroded away? What kind of professions might still be regarded as vocational? What about the social and moral dimensions of our political and social life? Above all, are these ultimately issues about God?

These are not narrowly political questions but broadly profound theological ones. For at the heart of our faith is the matter of simple and ultimate reality – a God whose concern is for promoting and sharing holiness, justice, peace and love. There is therefore an inescapable link between our human *togetherness* and the Kingdom of God. Does our experience of the particular context within which we work, and society in general, lead us to believe that the fabric of society is alerting and promoting people to care for their neighbour and share with their neighbours?

Who is going to guard, cherish and promote essential human well-being within society? Who has the vicarious task of judgement so that the pseudo divinities dominating culture and reducing human beings to functions are revealed for what they are? Priests and ministers have the privilege of meeting people in their flesh and blood, their living and dying, their suffering and recovering. These moments described movingly by many of the contributors are inescapably sacramental – they are to do with the sacredness and hallowing of ordinary things in ordinary people. We need therefore to look at ministry which will enable us to organize a life which the world can sustain and human beings can both endure and enjoy. Our authority as Christians comes from our common sense of calling and works only because we are human beings loved by God.

We are confronted by a pagan proletariat ... the mentality of their surroundings completely conquers them ... our mission must aim, not to organise those who already are practising Catholics ... but to penetrate the different milieu with the spirit of Christianity.[2]

As with our colleagues we think through these issues in the context of our own workplaces, we need to be reassured, challenged and drawn back to the metaphors that set us free. Above all, we need to be drawn back to the significance of the cross and resurrection of Jesus and to see that all human culture, including Christian culture, has to be revalued anew in their light.

Notes

1   Margaret Kane, *What Kind of God?* (London: SCM, 1986), p. 86.
2   Abbé Michonneau, *Reforming in a City Parish* (Oxford: Blackfriars, 1949), pp. 2 and 7.

Index